WARRANTIES
for Builders and
Remodelers

THIRD EDITION

David S. Jaffe
Felicia Watson
Zachary Packard

NAHB®
**National Association
of Home Builders**

Warranties for Builders and Remodelers, Third Edition
BuilderBooks, a Service of the National Association of Home Builders

Patricia Potts	Senior Director
Kristie McCauley	Copywriter
Design Central	Cover Design
Circle Graphics, Inc.	Composition
James W. Tobin III	NAHB Chief Executive Officer
John McGeary	NAHB SVP, Business Development
	& Brand Strategy

Disclaimer

Published in the United States of America

28 27 26 25 24   1 2 3 4 5

ISBN: 978-0-86718-815-8
eISBN: 978-0-86718-816-5

For further information, please contact:
National Association of Home Builders
1201 15th Street, NW
Washington, DC 20005-2800
BuilderBooks.com

CONTENTS

CONTENTS

FIGURES

FOREWORD

When I start meetings with home builders, I begin with *Warranties for Builders and Remodelers*. Builders and remodelers need to understand how the courts view their business. The exposure to the industry has evolved over the years, so a THIRD edition is warranted. To proactively address these risks, builders need to understand this background. Builders' potential exposure to litigation can have catastrophic consequences.

For decades, *Warranties for Builders and Remodelers* has been a must read for those of us in the industry. This book is an easy read, as it summarizes each state's statutes of repose and case law after several introductory chapters explaining express vs implied warranties, Alternative Dispute Resolution and other things of importance you need to know. You don't need to be a lawyer to read this.

I want to express my sincere thanks to the NAHB legal team. Turn the page for what builders and remodelers need to know.

James Leach, JD, MBA, CPCU
Executive Director
Maverick Insurance and Warranties

ABOUT THE AUTHORS

DAVID S. JAFFE is NAHB Staff Vice President, Construction Liability and Legal Research for the Office of Legal Affairs. He is the co-author of the fifth edition of *Contracts & Liability* and author of several other NAHB publications. He regularly advises the builder and remodeler members of NAHB on contract and liability issues and other aspects of construction law and risk management. He is a regular speaker at NAHB educational programs on contract and liability topics and trends related to the building industry.

FELICIA WATSON is NAHB Assistant Vice President, Construction Liability and Legal Research for the Office of Legal Affairs. She is the co-author of several other NAHB publications. Felicia works with builder and remodeler members of NAHB on contract, liability, and construction law. She also supports the Labor, Safety & Health group regarding OSHA and labor issues. Felicia is a frequent speaker at NAHB educational programs about various legal issues.

ZACH PACKARD is NAHB Staff Counsel for the Office of Legal Affairs, focusing on land use and advocacy. Zach works actively on member issues and potential litigation. A big part of his work is with NAHB's Legal Action Committee, which manages the NAHB Legal Action Fund. The Fund provides money to members who are either in active litigation or who will be filing litigation shortly and are facing issues of state or national significance.

INTRODUCTION

WARRANTY. A guarantee of the quality of the product and the warrantor's responsibility to repair or replace any defective parts.

". . . that defendant sold plaintiff a house with warranty, and that part of it, from its defective construction, had fallen in ruins, authorizes a recovery," *De Armas v. Gray*, 10 La. 575 (La. 1837). . . .

The 1837 Louisiana case cited above demonstrates that home construction warranties are not new, but the nature of home warranties, their use, and their prevalence has evolved and greatly expanded.

Builders originally only provided home construction warranties when a savvy purchaser could require warranty assurance from a constructing worker as part of the contract through negotiation and a superior bargaining position. At the time of *De Armas v. Gray*, builders were under no legal obligation to provide any warranty for home construction. Generally, they would not do so unless they had to provide a warranty to complete the sale of a house. The doctrine of *caveat emptor* (buyer beware) governed home construction and sales.

As competition for building, selling, and remodeling homes increased, builders and remodelers began offering written warranties as sales incentives or marketing tools. They voluntarily designed and proffered warranties to distinguish their skills and products from their competitors.

Following World War II as GIs returned to civilian life, the public's demand for new housing sharply escalated. Fueled by portrayals of fictional, "ideal" families on the radio and in the new medium of television, purchasing a home became synonymous with the American dream. The building industry responded with a surge in construction and development exemplified by the enormous Levittown, a Pennsylvania subdivision project that began in 1952.

Government entities began to view the assurance of new home quality as public policy to consider heeding the burgeoning expectations of the voting public. Thus, in the late 1950s and 1960s, American courts began to discard the ancient doctrine of *caveat emptor* in favor of a court-created doctrine called *implied warranty* for new home sales that imposed habitability and workmanlike construction requirements.

The current state of new home construction warranties continues to evolve. Some state legislatures have gone beyond the court-imposed implied warranties and have enacted statutory warranty requirements that codify specific construction standards, terms of warranty duration, claims procedures, and buyer remedies.

In today's business environment, building and remodeling professionals who actively seek a competitive edge provide construction warranties. Warranties can promote brand recognition, serve as a marketing tool, and a dispute resolution device. Whatever the motivation—from workmanship pride to mandatory state or federal requirements—the provision of home construction warranties is rising.

However, significant legal implications result from furnishing a warranty, implications that builders and remodelers may not fully understand. Therefore, the goal of this book is to provide home builders, remodelers, trade contractors, suppliers, and other industry professionals with vital knowledge concerning:

- The basic elements of a warranty.
- The different types of warranties.
- Drafting tips for warranties—sample language and formats.
- Potential legal pitfalls.
- Implied warranty requirements (state specific).
- Statutory warranty requirements (where applicable).
- Warranty claims procedures.
- Limitations on liability.

WARNING. The forms and procedures contained in this book are only illustrative. The authors are providing them for informational purposes only. Warranty law varies widely among states, and local municipal law may impose different requirements. Differences between the types of home construction projects, such as new home construction and remodeling, may affect the provisions of particular warranties. Draft your warranty agreements with great care and have a local attorney experienced in construction law review them.

1

EXPRESS WARRANTIES

An *express warranty* is the builder's or remodeler's (warrantor's) written or oral promise "expressly" made to the home buyer or homeowner (customer) that the work will meet specific standards and, if it does not, that the warrantor will stand behind the work by making repairs or by replacing defective components. The express warranty is part of the contract between the warrantor and the customer. The extent of a warrantor's responsibility to make repairs and to correct construction problems after the work is completed depends on the specific terms of the express warranty that the warrantor provides.

Written Versus Oral

A major motivation for warrantors to provide an express warranty is to give themselves a dispute-resolution mechanism for construction problems that may develop or be discovered subsequent to closing. A best practice is to provide a written express warranty to create a permanent, accurate record of the customer's rights and the warrantor's responsibilities. An oral warranty may generate disputes over its terms and conditions or whether an express warranty exists. Every time a builder, remodeler, or employee makes a statement regarding the quality of the work, or makes a remark about fixing problems after completion, the possibility of an express warranty is being extended. Without a permanent written record of the promise, the customer's expectations could differ from the builder's or remodeler's expectations. The builder or remodeler might be unaware of statements made by sales personnel or other employees that could be interpreted as an express warranty in a court of law.

A builder, remodeler, or employee creates an express warranty every time they make a statement regarding work quality.

Exclusive Warranty

The written warranty document includes an express warranty promise. However, other promises or legally imposed responsibilities can supplement or amend the written warranty. To avoid quality or customer service promises not covered in the written express warranty, acknowledge the written express warranty document is the sole and exclusive warranty provided by the warrantor. This situation can be avoided if, by its terms, the written express warranty document is acknowledged to be the sole and exclusive warranty provided by the warrantor. Any separate printed or oral statements or comments are not an amendment to the written express warranty document.

A Word of Caution. To avoid a claim of misrepresentation or a possible violation of the state's consumer protection laws, ensure that advertised promises do not conflict with the express written warranty terms.

Limited Warranty

It is a generally accepted practice to provide conditions or restrictions in express warranties that limit the extent of the warrantor's responsibility to the customer. The most common limits include conditions as to length of time that the warranty remains in effect, the specific components that are covered by the warranty, the extent of liability for damage, and the available methods for resolving disputes.

Time Restrictions. There is a point in time when residential occupants should reasonably be expected to have noticed most construction deficiencies, if any exist. And, there is a point in time when problems with a home's condition are more likely to be issues of maintenance than problems with the original construction. At either point, the warranty should cease, and responsibility for making home repairs should shift to the homeowner.

The duration of warranty coverage is specified in most express warranty documents. These periods can and do vary, but a one-year warranty duration is perhaps used the most. Some express warranties may provide for longer effective periods, particularly for specific components, such as mechanical, electrical, and plumbing (often two-year coverage); or foundations or load-bearing components (often five- or ten-year coverage).

Coverage. An express limited warranty generally restricts coverage to replacement or repair for defective workmanship or materials. It may further limit coverage to only latent (hidden) defects not apparent at occupancy. An express limited warranty should also specifically state which items or conditions are not covered. These nonwarranted items or conditions may include:

- Appliances covered by manufacturers' warranties.
- Exterior features such as landscaping or driveways.
- Damage caused by third parties or by the owner.
- Damage from acts of God, such as storms, floods, and fires.
- Damage resulting from the owner's failure to service and maintain.

Damage Exclusions. In some circumstances, a defective condition can lead to additional damage claims beyond the cost of the defect's repair. For example, a roof leak could cause damage to household furnishings, which is called *consequential damage.* Other indirect damage claims might include:

- Lodging expenses during repairs.
- Lost wages for time spent away from work.
- Payment for mental anguish.
- Medical bills and damage awards for personal injuries.
- Cost of inspections.
- Expenditures for third-party repairs.
- Legal fees.

An *express limited warranty* provides an opportunity to specifically exclude or to place monetary limits (caps) on any additional damage or expense claims that may arise as the result or consequence of a defect covered by an express warranty.

Dispute Resolution. Express warranty replacement and repair provisions can resolve disputes between the warrantor and customer, but disputes can still occur over issues like the adequacy of repairs or warranty coverage. A limited express warranty can specify the method of dispute resolution that may be employed, such as using mediation or binding arbitration rather than resorting to filing a lawsuit. A limited express warranty can also designate the procedures before initiating formal dispute resolution, such as requiring a notice to a warrantor of a claimed defect and providing an opportunity to inspect a defect and to make a repair.

Warning. The forms and procedures contained in this book are illustrative. The authors are providing them for information purposes only. Warranty law varies widely among states, and local municipal law may impose different requirements. Differences between the types of home construction projects, such as new home construction and remodeling, may affect the provisions of particular warranties. Draft your warranty agreements with great care and have a local attorney experienced in construction law review them. Sample disclaimer language used in this book is for informational purposes only. It is not suitable for every jurisdiction.

2

IMPLIED WARRANTIES

In addition to the express warranties that builders knowingly and deliberately provide for new home construction, hidden or implied warranties are imposed primarily by state court rulings or occasionally by statute, and they affect new home builder-vendors.

The work of a remodeler on an existing home does not typically subject the remodeler to liability under an implied warranty for new home construction. However, in at least one state (Illinois), an implied warranty is imposed on the construction of a major addition to an existing home. The work of a trade contractor on a new home does not make the trade contractor liable to the property owner under an implied warranty for new home construction. However, the general contractor (builder) is responsible for the work of the trade contractors, and the builder will be liable under an implied warranty for that work—even though the trade contractors are not.

However, remodelers and trade contractors may not be exempt from all implied warranty liability. Other implied warranties could apply to them under certain circumstances. Many courts hold that whenever someone claims to be specially qualified to do a particular type of work, that person is subject to an implied warranty that (a) the work will be done in a workmanlike manner, and (b) the resulting construction will be reasonably fit for its intended use.

What happened to the doctrine of *caveat emptor*? As late as 1957, the courts for all the states consistently held that without an express warranty, a home buyer had no redress for faulty construction, i.e., let the buyer beware. However, the dynamics of home construction changed in the twentieth century. Homes became more complicated in their construction, design, and features. Adding new heating, electrical, and plumbing systems and insulation, the use of new building materials and components, and the mass production of homes using subcontracted labor all added to the complexity of home construction.

Courts began to recognize that an ordinary purchaser lacked the expertise to determine whether a new home was of sound construction. As the cost of a new home became more and more expensive (a typical family's single greatest financial commitment), state courts began to listen to the argument that builder-vendors, who were perceived as construction experts, should bear more responsibility for delivering a high-quality product. One by one, the courts decreed that for new home purchases, the doctrine of *caveat emptor* was fundamentally unfair and against public policy. Today, it is now widely accepted, that the builder-vendor of a new dwelling impliedly warrants that the property is habitable and fit for its intended purpose as a residence.

These implied warranties are generally of two types. The implied warranty of habitability provides that a new home must be sufficiently safe and sound to be actually lived in and to serve its function as a residence. The implied warranty of workmanlike construction goes beyond the issue of habitability and provides that the workmanship must meet the standards of quality that prevail at the time and place of construction. These implied warranties pertain only to latent defects, defined as problems with the work or the building materials that are not discovered, nor reasonably discoverable, at the time of closing. Courts also require these latent defects to be of a significant nature such that they affect the use or livability of a home. However, the current trend in court decisions is to lessen the latent defect's required degree of significance.

Building code violations are matters separate and apart. Certainly, code violations, if the condition is latent, may constitute a breach of the implied warranty of habitability or workmanlike construction. However, a house can pass all code requirements and still have latent defects that are subject to liability under implied warranties.

Originally, courts imposed implied warranties only for the benefit of the original new home purchaser. They ruled that to benefit from an implied warranty, the home owner had to have a direct contractual relationship with the builder-vendor under a doctrine called *privity of contract*.

In 1976 the Indiana Supreme Court became the first state court to extend implied warranties to subsequent purchasers. It dispensed with the privity of contract doctrine in favor of the "public policy" consideration that a new home should be habitable and of workmanlike construction regardless of who the present owner might be. Not all states have abandoned privity of contract, but the trend among state courts appears to be in that direction.

Sample Case Law

NEW JERSEY. *McDonald v. Mianecki,* 398 A.2d 1283 (N.J. 1979). The doctrine of implied warranty of habitability applies to the construction of new homes by builders-vendors whether or not they are mass developers. The implied warranty of habitability encompasses the potability of water.

WASHINGTON. *Stuart v. Coldwell Banker Commercial Group, Inc.,* 745 P.2d 1284 (Wash. 1987). The doctrine of implied warranty of habitability imposes liability upon builders-vendors in favor of original purchasers of residential property for egregious defects in the fundamental structure of the home. The implied warranty of habitability does not provide recovery for defects in exterior, nonstructural elements adjacent to the dwelling unit (such as private decks and walkways).

ILLINOIS. *VonHoldt v. Barba & Barba Construction, Inc.,* 677 N.E.2d 836 (Ill. 1997). The court noted that it had previously held that the doctrine of implied warranty of habitability did not apply to the refurbishing and renovation of existing homes. The court observed that this ruling applied where the project had not been significant. The court distinguished the circumstances in the present case because the builder had constructed a multilevel addition to an existing home, increasing the size of the original house by 40 percent. The court held that, when a builder makes a significant addition to a previously built home, an action for latent defects exists under the doctrine of implied warranty of habitability.

MASSACHUSETTS. *Albrecht v. Clifford,* 767 N.E.2d 42 (Mass. 2002). The court noted that the implied warranty of habitability that attaches to the sale of new homes by builders-vendors does not make the builder an insurer against any and all defects in a home. The court held that to establish a breach of implied warranty of habitability, the home owner must demonstrate that (a) a new house was purchased from a builder-vendor; (b) the house contained a latent defect that manifested itself only after purchase; (c) the defect was caused by the builder's improper design, material, or workmanship; and (d) the defect was not trivial or aesthetic but posed a substantial question of safety or made the house unfit for human habitation.

NEBRASKA. *Moglia v. McNeil Company, Inc.,* 700 N.W.2d 608 (Neb. 2005). Subcontractors are not liable to property owners for any breach of implied duty to perform in a workmanlike manner. Unlike subcontractors, general contractors are liable to new homeowners under the implied warranty of workmanlike performance. On the basis of public policy, the court rules that privity should not be required between a remote purchaser and a general contractor with respect to the implied warranty of workmanship and habitability. The implied warranty imposed on general contractors for new home construction is therefore extended to subsequent purchasers. Liability is limited to latent defects that (a) manifest themselves after the subsequent purchase and (b) that are not discoverable at the time of subsequent purchase by reasonably prudent inspection.

IOWA. *Speight v. Walter Development Co., Ltd,* 744 N.W.2d 108 (Iowa 2008). Holding that Iowa law should follow the emerging and better view that subsequent purchasers may recover against a builder-vendor for a breach of the implied warranty of workmanlike construction. The subsequent purchaser is in no better position to discover those defects than the original purchaser and thus it would be inequitable to allow an original purchaser to recover while, simultaneously, prohibiting a subsequent purchaser from recovering for latent defects in homes that are the same age. Moreover, the builder-vendor's risk is not increased by allowing subsequent purchasers to recover for the same latent defects for which an original purchaser could recover. Subsequent purchasers, of course, may not be afforded greater rights of recovery than the original purchasers.

UTAH. *Davencourt at Pilgrims Landing Homeowners Ass'n v. Davencourt at Pilgrims Landing LC,* 221 P.3d 324 (Utah 2009). In Utah, the scope of the implied warranty should be construed broadly to comport with the public policy considerations. To establish a breach of the implied warranty of workmanlike manner or habitability under Utah law a plaintiff must show (1) the purchase of a new residence from a defendant builder-vendor/developer-vendor; (2) the residence contained a latent defect; (3) the defect manifested itself after purchase; (4) the defect was caused by improper design, material, or workmanship; and (5) the defect created a question of safety or made the house unfit for human habitation.

VERMONT. *Long Trail House Condominium Association v. Engelberth Construction, Inc.,* 59 A.3d 752 (Vt. 2012). The court concluded that, where the implied warranty is deemed to arise out of a contract of sale, it cannot be extended to a second purchaser. The court reasoned that, because there is no sales agreement between the builder-vendor and the second purchaser and hence no privity of contract, there can be no implied warranty. The litigation stemmed from the construction of a 143–unit condominium complex known as the Long Trail House at Stratton Mountain, Vermont. The Association's implied warranty claims rested on the construction contract between the general contractor and the owner, Stratton Corporation. It argued that these implied warranties were included as part of the contract between general contractor and Stratton, and that it was entitled to bring this cause of action because such warranties "pass from a developer to a subsequent purchaser." The court rejected this argument, finding that pursuant to Vermont case law the existence of implied warranties in these cases, and the rationale underlying them, are founded on a sale, and there was no sale between Engelberth and the Association here.

PENNSYLVANIA. *Conway v. Cutler Group, Inc.,* 99 A.3d 67 (Pa. 2014). The issue presented in this case was whether a builder's implied warranty of habitability, which protects those who purchase a newly constructed home from latent defects, could also be invoked by subsequent purchasers of the home. The court held that a subsequent purchaser of a previously inhabited residence may not recover contract damages for breach of the builder's implied warranty of habitability. In a case of first impression, the court looked to decisions from other states that had addressed it and concluded that they had reached varying resolutions. After careful review, the court concluded that the question of whether and/or under what circumstances to extend an implied warranty of habitability to subsequent purchasers of a newly constructed residence is a matter of public policy properly left to the General Assembly.

CHAPTER 3

DISCLAIMERS

U nder certain circumstances and for various reasons, a builder or remodeler may want to disclaim all warranties. For example, a remodeler hired to finish or repair someone else's work may disclaim all warranties, so the remodeler is not responsible for deficiencies in the original construction. Or a disclaimer of warranties could be a price factor. For example, to receive a rock-bottom price, a client may waive all warranties to avoid paying for warranty coverage to pay the least amount possible. Acceptance of the work in "as is" condition is one example of a disclaimer of all warranties.

Disclaimers of Implied Warranties

Builder-vendors, particularly those who provide express limited warranties to their customers, may also want to disclaim the implied warranties that apply to the sale of new homes. Implied warranty law is subject to vague and unpredictable interpretations that can vary from one court decision to another. Courts often disagree on whether a home is habitable, on what constitutes an implied warranty defect, and on what are the prevailing standards of construction for a specific locality. Builders and home buyers are both left to guess the extent of their rights and responsibilities. Lacking clear guidance, a builder's and a home buyer's expectations can differ, and it may take a lawsuit to sort the matter out. Using an express limited warranty that disclaims all implied warranties eliminates this uncertainty and confusion.

The duration of liability is another reason that a builder may want to disclaim an implied warranty. Homeowners should have the opportunity to live in their homes and notice whether any problems develop that were not apparent at closing. Over time, the quality of the builder's original construction becomes less central to the home's current condition and will be overshadowed by the homeowner's maintenance responsibilities.

Builders are businessmen and businesswomen, and open-ended liability of indefinite duration is not a sound business practice. It can directly affect the:

- Solvency of the business.
- Cost of insuring the business.
- Cost of home construction.
- Affordability of homes.

Imposing a cut-off period for further builder repairs is reasonable. Such repair limitations have long been used in the automotive industry and are generally accepted by the public. Reasonable limits on the duration of warranties and builder liability should be just as acceptable in the home building industry.

Most implied warranties for new home construction have no stated duration and are subject to cut-off only through the application of a statute of limitations.[1]

A statute of limitations is a law that limits the time a person must file a claim in court. The length of time (generally several years) depends on the type of claim, and the time can vary considerably. For example, a breach of contract claim may have a different limitations period than a breach of duty claim (negligence). Each state has its own statute of limitations. Many states have a statute of limitations period for construction defect claims. However, the periods provided in the states' statutes of limitations have no uniformity.

Perhaps most surprising is the fact that under certain circumstances the time period in a state's statute of limitations will not apply. For latent defect claims, the period for bringing a claim may actually extend indefinitely. Why? Because the statute of limitations is suspended (tolled) until the homeowner actually discovers the latent problem or defect or until a court determines that the homeowner reasonably should have discovered it or known that damage had occurred. This discovery rule means that there is no upper limit on the amount of time that a statute of limitations may be tolled.

However, if the state has a statute of repose, there may be relief from indefinite liability. This statute provides an absolute cut-off time a person must bring suit on a claim, regardless of when the claimant discovers the problem. Most, but not all, states have statutes of repose. However, these statutes generally provide for an extended period before all claims

---

1. Virginia Code Ann. § 55-70.1, a statutory provision of implied warranties for new home construction includes express duration limits.

are barred. The average cut-off time among state statutes of repose for construction-related claims is around ten years. (See Appendix A for a list of the statutes of repose for each state.)

A builder-vendor who has provided a customer with a one-year limited express warranty may be astonished to learn that a remaining potential liability threat might last for ten years (or more). This lengthy duration of implied warranties makes the one-year limitations period under the builder's-vendor's express warranty virtually meaningless unless the implied warranties are disclaimed and waived.

However, disclaiming an implied warranty is not necessarily an easy task. The courts created implied warranties for new home construction on public policy grounds. Even though most states permit implied warranties to be waived and disclaimed, the courts do not favor that action, and attempts to disclaim implied warranties will be strictly construed against the builder.[2]

While the Arizona state Supreme Court recently held that a disclaimer of implied warranty of workmanship and habitability was void as contrary to public policy. *See Zambrano v M & RC II LLC*, 517 P.3d 1168 (Ariz. 2022). See also decisions in Texas and Massachusetts, where courts in those states have held, also on public policy grounds, that a disclaimer of the implied warranty of habitability is not permitted, and it also cannot be waived. *Centex Homes v. Buecher*, 95 S.W.3d 266 (Texas 2002); *Albrecht v. Clifford*, 767 N.E.2d 42 (Mass. 2002). Courts hold that, to be effective, a waiver of an implied warranty must be clearly stated in unambiguous language and must be voluntarily agreed to by the purchaser.

Note that waiver language proven to be effective in one state may be ineffective as a disclaimer in another. Some states consider the simple phrase "as is" to be an enforceable disclaimer of implied warranties, but in other states, the waiver requirements can be quite stringent, including:

- Specific waiver language.
- Separate signatures.
- Specific references by name to the individual implied warranties that are to be waived.
- A specific contract location requirement for disclaimer language (or at least the waiver clause has a prominent place in the contract).
- The use of a certain type and font size.
- Specific insurance coverage (For example, see the excerpt from the *Annotated Indiana Code* in Figure 3.1.).

For other examples of sample disclaimers, see Figures 3.2 and 3.3.

---

2. In North Dakota the state Supreme Court has held that all warranties may properly be excluded, but that exclusion must be part of the bargain between the parties. *See Leno v. K&L Homes, Inc.*, 803 N.W.2d 543 (ND 2011).

FIGURE **3.1**

Sample Disclaimer of Implied Warranties from Annotated Indiana Code

TITLE 32. PROPERTY

ARTICLE 27. CONSTRUCTION WARRANTIES ON REAL PROPERTY

CHAPTER 2. NEW HOME CONSTRUCTION WARRANTIES
32-27-2-9 Disclaimer of implied warranties

Sec. 9. (a) A builder may disclaim all implied warranties only if all of the following conditions are met:

(1) The warranties defined in this chapter are expressly provided for in the written contract between a builder and an initial home buyer of a new home.
(2) The performance of the warranty obligations is backed by an insurance policy in an amount at least equal to the purchase price of the new home.
(3) The builder carries completed operations products liability insurance covering the builder's liability for reasonably foreseeable consequential damages arising from a defect covered by the warranties provided by the builder.
   (b) The disclaimer must be printed in a minimum size of 10-point boldface type setting forth that the statutory warranties of this chapter are in lieu of the implied warranties that have been disclaimed by the builder, and the initial home buyer must affirmatively acknowledge by complete signature that the home buyer has read, understands, and voluntarily agrees to the disclaimer. Additionally, the initial home buyer must acknowledge the disclaimer of implied warranties by signing, at the time of execution of the contract, a separate one (1) page notice, attached to the contract, that includes and begins with the following language:

"NOTICE OF WAIVER OF IMPLIED WARRANTIES"

I recognize that by accepting the express warranties and the insurance covering those warranties for the periods of time provided in this contract, I am giving up the right to any claims for implied warranties, which may be greater than the express warranties. Implied warranties are unwritten warranties relating to the reasonable expectations of a homeowner regarding the construction of the homeowner's home, as those reasonable expectations are defined by the courts on a case-by-case basis."

   (c) If there is a default of either:
      (1) the insurance for the performance of the warranty obligations; or
      (2) the completed operations products liability insurance; the disclaimer by the builder is void from and after the default.

FIGURE
3.2

Sample Disclaimer—Waiver of All Implied Warranties

The parties acknowledge that the terms of the express, written warranty provided herein by the seller constitute the buyer's sole and exclusive remedy for any and all claims arising out of defects in materials or construction. Any implied warranties, including an implied warranty of workmanlike construction, an implied warranty of habitability, or an implied warranty of fitness for a particular use, are hereby waived and disclaimed.

I acknowledge receipt of the notice, disclosure, and disclaimer agreement. I have carefully read and reviewed its terms, and I agree to its provisions.

_____	_____	_____	_____
(Buyer)	(Date)	(Seller)	(Date)

_____	_____	_____	_____
(Buyer)	(Date)	(Seller)	(Date)

Most state courts have not directly addressed the issue of whether disclaimers agreed to between a builder and an original purchaser are enforceable against a subsequent purchaser. However, this very issue was addressed by the Supreme Court of Illinois in *Fattah v. Bim*, 52 N.E.3d 332 (Ill. 2016). The court addressed the question of whether the implied warranty of habitability may be extended to a second purchaser of a house when a valid, bargained-for waiver of the warranty was executed between the builder-vendor and the first purchaser? The court explained that it is not a given that the implied warranty may be extended to a second purchaser when a waiver of the warranty exists. Here, the subsequent purchaser was not simply seeking to recover those damages that would have been available to the first purchaser of the house, under the implied warranty of habitability, but instead, because the first purchaser waived the implied warranty, the subsequent purchaser was seeking to recover more than what the first purchaser would have been entitled to. If the implied warranty is extended to a second purchaser even in the face of a valid waiver, the financial certainty, which the builder-vendor bargained for and assumed it had obtained, is lost. The builder-vendor has no means of knowing when the house might be sold by the first purchaser or to whom and, thus, no way of knowing when, or if, liability for latent defects in the construction of the house will reappear.

FIGURE
3.3

Sample Disclaimer of "As Is" Conveyance—Waiver of Implied Warranties

The parties acknowledge that the home being purchased is conveyed "as is" without warranty, express or implied. Any implied warranties, including an implied warranty of workmanlike construction, an implied warranty of habitability, or an implied warranty of fitness for a particular use, are hereby waived and disclaimed.

    I acknowledge receipt of the notice, disclosure, and disclaimer agreement. I have carefully read and reviewed its terms, and I agree to its provisions.

_____   _____   _____   _____

(Buyer)   (Date)   (Seller)   (Date)

_____   _____   _____   _____

(Buyer)   (Date)   (Seller)   (Date)

Because builders and remodelers cannot easily disclaim implied warranties, and because state laws affecting disclaimers vary tremendously, builders and remodelers should consult with a local attorney (a) to determine the validity of an implied warranty waiver in their jurisdictions and (b) to draft the appropriate language in a format that will make such a disclaimer enforceable. Builders and remodelers should not attempt to draft their disclaimer instruments.

Sample Case Law

The effectiveness of purported disclaimers and waivers of implied warranties for new home construction and sales is a frequently litigated issue. Some recent representative case decisions follow.

CONNECTICUT. *Cafro v. Brophy*, 774 A.2d 206 (Conn. App. Ct. 2001). Conn. Gen. Stat. 47-118(d) expressly provides that an effective disclaimer must set forth in detail the warranty to be excluded. The court holds that a disclaimer in the contract for the sale of a new home stating that "all warranties are excluded" tells the buyer absolutely nothing, falls far short of statutory compliance, and is void.

ILLINOIS. *Village Centre Condo. Ass'n., Inc., v. Wilmette Partners* 760 N.E.2d. 976 (Ill. 2001). A knowing disclaimer of the implied warranty of habitability is not against public policy, although such a disclaimer will be strictly construed against the builder. The disclaimer must be conspicuous and must fully disclose its consequences, and the parties must voluntarily agree to it. Given that an implied warranty of habitability is distinct from other warranties, the court held that a "waiver of all implied warranties" is not a valid disclaimer because it does not refer to a waiver of the implied warranty of habitability by name.

VIRGINIA. *Speier v. Renaissance Housing Corporation,* 58 Va. Cir. 90 (2001). Virginia code section 55-70.1 permits the waiver of implied warranties, provided that the disclaimer language is in capital letters that are at least two points larger than the other type in the contract. The waiver terms in the parties' contract were plainly set forth and were in capital letters. But, because the font size did not exceed the other type by at least two points, the waiver was void.

ALABAMA. *Turner v. Westhampton Court, LLC,* 903 So. 2d 82 (Ala. 2004). A one-year express warranty given by the vendor and signed by the purchasers included text set off in a box from the rest of the document in capital letters in a font larger than the rest of the text. It stated in pertinent part, "This warranty is given in lieu of any and all other warranties, either express or implied, including any implied warranty of merchantability, fitness for a particular purpose, habitability, and workmanship." The court ruled that it was a valid, enforceable disclaimer.

NORTH CAROLINA. *Bass v. Pinnacle Custom Homes, Inc.,* 592 S.E.2d 606 (N.C. Ct. App. 2004). Purchasers had waived implied warranty of habitability on a newly constructed home. At closing, they had accepted an express limited warranty stating, "all other warranties, express or implied, including but not limited to any implied warranty of habitability, are hereby disclaimed and waived. This express warranty is the sole warranty of the parties, and no one can add to or vary the terms of this express warranty."

TENNESSEE. *Campbell v. Teague,* 2010 W.L. 1240732 (Tenn Ct. App., March 31, 2010). The inclusion of a one-year builder's warranty is not sufficient to waive the warranties implied in law.

NORTH DAKOTA. *Leno v. K&L Homes, Inc.,* 803 N.W.2d 543 (N.D. 2011). K & L Homes had not, as a matter of law, disclaimed any implied warranties through the Homeowners' Guide the Lenos received at closing. The court explained that the attempted disclaimer was ineffective because it was given at closing and was not a part of the basis of the bargain between the parties.

OHIO. *Jones v. Centex Homes*, 967 N.E.2d 1199 (Ohio 2012). The sole question before the court was whether a home buyer can waive his right to enforce a home builder's legal duty to construct a house in a workman-like manner. The court held that he cannot.

PENNSYLVANIA. *Krishnan v. The Cutler Group*, 171 A.3d 856 (Pa. Super. Ct. 2017). This case arose out of a complaint that the builder improperly constructed the home, which resulted in chronic water infiltration and damage to the home. The purchasers alleged that the language in the Warranty did not mention 'habitability' or 'reasonable workmanship.' It simply used the generic term 'implied warranties.' Thus, the language did not provide them with adequate notice of the specific implied warranty protections they were purportedly waiving by signing the Warranty. The court agreed, concluding that the implied warranties of habitability and reasonable workmanship were not properly limited by the builder.

Builders and remodelers should not attempt to draft their own disclaimer instruments.

Warning. Sample disclaimer language is for information only. It is not suitable for every jurisdiction.

CHAPTER 4

THE WARRANTY DOCUMENT

A warranty is a type of contract. As with other contracts, warranty terms and conditions should be clear, concise, and in writing. Typically, the builder or remodeler voluntarily provides the warranty to the homeowner. As provider, the builder or remodeler is free to determine the terms of the warranty, so long as they conform to any local, state, or federal requirements. To avoid confusion and to manage expectations, the prudent warrantor will comprehensively set forth the essential warranty terms in the warranty document provided to the homeowner. Figure 4.1 identifies the primary items that the warranty should address.

Failure to abide by warranty provisions may subject a builder or remodeler to a breach of warranty claim by a homeowner. To avoid these types of claims, the builder or remodeler should not make any unintended promises or representations regarding the quality of the work or what happens if a defect occurs. Your attorney should review all brochures, advertising, or other marketing devices for representations that may seem like warranties. In addition, builders and remodelers should consider adding language found in the following sample acknowledging transmittal and acceptance of their warranty documents.

FIGURE 4.1

Essential Elements of a Warranty

A. Names and Addresses
  1. Home buyer(s) or owner(s)
  2. Builder or remodeler
B. Scope of Warranty—Questions to Consider
  1. What is covered?
    a. Design
    b. Materials
    c. Workmanship
    d. Latent defects (define)
  2. What is not covered?
    a. Consumer products (for purposes of the Magnuson-Moss Warranty Act)
    b. Damage caused by ordinary wear and tear
    c. Damage resulting from neglect by the owner or the owner's failure to provide proper maintenance
    d. Defects in items installed by the owner or someone other than the builder
    e. Any existing trees or other landscaping
    f. Damage caused by acts of God or nature
    g. Items expressly listed as non-warrantable
    h. [Include a warning that the list of items not covered is not exclusive.]
  3. What constitutes a defect? What standards will you incorporate into your warranty?
    a. Industry guidelines
    b. Local guidelines prepared by your local home builders association
    c. A local model building code or the International Building Code
    d. NAHB's Residential Construction Performance Guidelines (see Resources)
C. Term of Warranty
  1. What is the commencement date of the warranty?
  2. When is the closing?
  3. When is occupancy allowed?
  4. Is the warranty invalid if payment is outstanding under a mortgage?
  5. What is the duration of the express warranty—one, two, five, or more years?
  6. What is the duration of the implied warranty? Is it limited to the duration of the express warranty? If not, what is it? [Acknowledge that some states do not allow limitation of implied warranties.]
D. Remedies
  1. Do you want to claim the builder's or remodeler's option to repair or replace or pay for either?
  2. Will you limit payment of incidental or consequential damages?
  3. Will you limit recovery of damages for emotional distress, mental anguish, and the like?
  4. Will you provide for liquidated damages?
  5. Will you include a place for the owner's acknowledgment (by initialing the statement) of limitations?
E. Claims Procedure
  1. Will you require written notice of defects, except for emergencies, and provide for emergency reports by telephone, fax, or e-mail?

(continued)

FIGURE **4.1**

Essential Elements of a Warranty (*Continued*)

  2. Will you provide for inspection of the problems and include a response time (30 days)?
  3. Will you include
     a. A response time for the necessary repairs (90 days)?
     b. A disclaimer for delays for reasons beyond the builder's or remodeler's control?
     c. A statement that repairs will be done during normal working hours and state those hours?
F. No Additional Warranty
G. Transferability
  1. Will you limit the warranty to the owner while he or she occupies the residence?
  2. If not, does the owner need your prior written consent to assign or transfer the warranty to a subsequent purchaser of the house?
H. Owner's Acknowledgment of Receipt of Warranty
  1. Will you ask the owner to sign and date the warranty document to acknowledge receipt of the warranty?
I. Manufacturer's Warranties
  1. Will you assign the manufacturers' warranties to the owner if the manufacturer permits such a transfer?
  2. Will your warranty trigger the requirements of the Magnuson-Moss Act? If so, does the warranty comply with the act?

Warning. This list is for information and planning only and is not necessarily comprehensive.

Sample Language—Acknowledgment of Transmittal and Acceptance of Warranty

1. The buyer has thoroughly examined the residential property to be conveyed that is described herein;
2. The buyer has received, has read, and understands this limited warranty; and
3. Neither the builder, nor the builder's representatives, have made any guarantees, warranties, understandings, or representations that are not set forth in this document.

I acknowledge having read, understood, and received a copy of this limited warranty agreement.

| _____ | _____ | _____ |
| (Buyer) | (Builder) | (Date) |

Builders and remodelers should educate salespeople and other parties that they authorize to speak to homeowners on their behalf regarding their warranty provisions. They also should monitor them periodically to determine whether these representatives' promises are consistent with the warranty. For extra protection, the builder's or remodeler's subcontracts should expressly prohibit a trade contractor from making any representations or promises on the guarantor's behalf to the owner.

Builders and remodelers should educate all parties that they authorize to speak to homeowners on their behalf regarding their warranty provisions.

To implement these strategies, builders and remodelers should consult with their attorneys. An attorney who is well versed in contract and construction law can provide valuable assistance by reviewing the warranty documents and all marketing materials to assure that that (a) they comply with any applicable laws or regulations and (b) contain no unintended promises or representations. The attorney's knowledge and experience would be particularly advisable for drafting the warranty document because of the complexity of conforming with the Magnuson-Moss Act, state statutory provisions, and the dictates of case law decisions. During the period of the warranty service plan, the services of an attorney may also be valuable in the interpretation of any uncertain claim situations.

Sample Warranty Forms

The sample warranty forms in Figures 4.2–4.4 are provided for information only. They have not been crafted for use in any specific jurisdiction. You can find many versions of express warranties, and only a few examples are included here. The forms provided herein may not conform to the specific requirements of a particular state's laws concerning new home warranties or home-improvement warranties. Builders and remodelers should consult a local attorney to assist in drafting their warranties with utmost care.

FIGURE 4.2

Sample Builder's Limited Warranty Agreement
(Excluding Items Covered by the Magnuson-Moss Act)

This limited warranty agreement is extended by _____ (the builder), whose address is _____, to the original buyer _____ (the buyer) of the residential property located at the following address:

_____

_____

_____

This limited warranty excludes consequential damages, limits the duration of implied warranties, and provides for liquidated damages.

1. WHAT IS COVERED BY THE WARRANTY

The builder warrants that all construction related to the house substantially conforms to the plans and specifications and change orders for this job. The builder warrants that during the first thirty (30) days after occupancy by the buyer, the builder will, after inspection of the property, adjust or correct observable defects or omissions (such as missing equipment or hardware; sticking doors, drawers, and windows; dripping faucets; and other reported malfunctions).

Within one (1) year from the date of closing or occupancy by the buyer, whichever is first, the builder will repair or replace, at the builder's option, any latent defects, not apparent or ascertainable at the time of occupancy, in the building materials or workmanship as defined by the standards of construction set out in the current edition of the Residential Construction Performance Guidelines (see Resources). The buyer agrees to accept reasonable matches in any repair or replacement in the event the specified or originally used item is no longer available.

2. WHAT IS NOT COVERED

This limited warranty does not cover the following items:

A. Damage resulting from fires, floods, storms, electrical malfunctions, accidents, or acts of God.

B. Damage from alterations, misuse, or abuse of the covered items by any person.

C. Damage resulting from the home buyer's failure to perform reasonable home maintenance.

D. Damage resulting from the buyer's failure to observe any operating instructions furnished by the builder at the time of installation.

E. Damage resulting from a malfunction of equipment or lines of the telephone, gas, power, or water companies.

F. Any items listed as non-warrantable conditions on the list that is incorporated into this contract. The buyer acknowledges receipt of the statement of nonwarrantable conditions. _____
   (buyer's initials)

(*continued*)

FIGURE 4.2

**Sample Builder's Limited Warranty Agreement
(Excluding Items Covered by the Magnuson-Moss Act)
(*Continued*)**

G. Any item furnished or installed by the buyer.
H. Any appliance, piece of equipment, or other item that is a consumer product for the purposes of the Magnuson-Moss Warranty Act, 15 United States Code §§ 2301 et seq., installed or included in the buyer's property. Examples of consumer products include, but are not limited to, dishwasher, garbage disposal, gas or electric range, range hood, refrigerator, microwave oven, trash compactor, garage door opener, washer, dryer, water heater, furnace, or heat pump. The only warranties for any appliance, pieces of equipment, or other items considered to be a consumer product for the purposes of the Magnuson Moss Act are those provided by the products' manufacturers.

    (1) The builder has made any manufacturers' warranties available to the buyer for inspection, and the buyer acknowledges receipt of these warranties, as requested.

    _____
    (buyer's initials)

    (2) The builder hereby assigns (to the extent that they are assignable) and conveys to the buyer all warranties provided to the builder on any manufactured items that have been installed or included in the buyer's property. The buyer accepts this assignment and acknowledges that the builder's only responsibility relating to such items is to lend assistance to the buyer in settling any claim resulting from the installation of these products.

    _____   _____
    (buyer's initials)   (builder's initials)

3. REMEDIES AND LIMITATIONS

A. The buyer understands that the sole remedies under this limited warranty agreement are repair and replacement, as set forth herein.

    _____
    (buyer's initials)

B. With respect to any future claim whatsoever that may be asserted by the buyer against the builder or the builder's employees, the buyer understands that the buyer will have no right to recover, or to request compensation for, and the builder shall not be liable for any of the following:

    (1) Incidental, consequential, secondary, or punitive damages
    (2) Damages for aggravation, mental anguish, emotional distress, or pain and suffering
    (3) Attorney's fees or costs

    _____
    (buyer's initials)

(*continued*)

FIGURE

Sample Builder's Limited Warranty Agreement
(Excluding Items Covered by the Magnuson-Moss Act)
(*Continued*)

C. **The builder hereby limits the duration of all implied warranties, including the implied warranties of habitability, and workmanlike construction to one (1) year from the date of sale or the date of occupancy, whichever comes first. The buyer specifically agrees to this limitation.**

————————————
(buyer's initials)

These limitations shall be enforceable to the extent permitted by law.

(Some states do not allow the exclusion or limitation of incidental or consequential damages or the limitation of implied warranties, so the limitations or exclusions listed above may not apply in a particular location.)

(Alternative to 3C)

C. **The buyer understands and agrees that no implied warranties whatsoever apply to the structure of the house or to items that are functionally part of the house. The builder disclaims, and the buyer waives, any implied warranties, including, but not limited to, the implied warranty of habitability, the implied warranty of workmanlike construction, and the implied warranty of fitness for a particular purpose. These limitations shall be enforceable to the extent permitted by the law.**

————————————
(buyer's initials)

(Some states do not allow disclaimers of the implied warranty of habitability; other states may require such disclaimers to use specific language, type size, and format.)

D. Notwithstanding the provisions of this limited warranty agreement, if any liability arises on the part of the builder, the builder will pay only the amount of actual provable damages arising from such liability, but, in any event, this amount shall not exceed $_____. This amount, fixed as liquidated damages and not as a penalty, shall be the builder's complete and exclusive amount of liability. The provisions of this paragraph apply if loss or damage results directly or indirectly to persons or property from the performance of, or failure to perform, obligations imposed by the construction contract or from negligence, active or otherwise, of the builder or the builder's agents or employees.

The buyer (a) understands that this provision limits the damages for which the builder will be liable and (b) acknowledges acceptance of this liquidated damages provision in consideration for the limited warranties provided by the builder and the other provisions of the construction contract. Therefore, the owner buyer agrees to these

(*continued*)

FIGURE **4.2**

Sample Builder's Limited Warranty Agreement
(Excluding Items Covered by the Magnuson-Moss Act)
(*Continued*)

liquidated damages clause if, notwithstanding the provisions of this limited warranty, liability should arise on the part of the builder. _____
(buyer's initials)

E. This warranty is personal to the original buyer and does not run with the property or with the items contained in the house. The original buyer may not assign, transfer, or convey this warranty without the prior written consent of the builder. _____
(buyer's initials)

4. HOW TO OBTAIN SERVICE

If a problem develops during the warranty period, the buyer must notify the builder of the specific problem in writing delivered to the builder at the address specified herein. This written statement of the problem must include the buyer's name, address, telephone number, e-mail address, and a description of the nature of the problem. Within a reasonable time of receipt, the builder will inspect to determine if the problem is covered under this warranty. If covered, the builder will perform the repair or replacement obligations under this warranty within a reasonable time and will diligently pursue this obligation.

Repair work will be done during the builder's normal working hours, except in emergency situations where delay may cause additional damage. The buyer agrees to provide the builder or builder's representative access to the house for all inspections and repairs. The buyer also agrees to be present or to have present a responsible adult with authority to authorize the repair and to sign an acceptance-of-repair ticket upon completion.

5. WHERE TO GET HELP

For information concerning this warranty, the buyer should contact the builder's customer service representative at

_____
(name, address, phone number, fax number, e-mail address)

Any notice or other document required or permitted to be delivered under this warranty, including written statements of problems, may be sent by first class mail to these authorized individuals at their addresses listed below.

_____   _____
(Name)   (Address)

_____   _____
(Name)   (Address)

(*continued*)

FIGURE 4.2

Sample Builder's Limited Warranty Agreement
(Excluding Items Covered by the Magnuson-Moss Act)
(*Continued*)

6. THE ONLY WARRANTY GIVEN BY THE BUILDER—EXCLUSIVE REMEDY

(a) The buyer has thoroughly examined the residential property described herein that is to be conveyed, (b) the buyer has received, has read, and understands this limited warranty, and (c) neither the builder, nor the builder's representatives, have made any guarantees, warranties, understandings, or representations that are not set forth in this document. This warranty document constitutes the exclusive remedy of all claims by the buyer against the builder or the builder's employees. The buyer specifically waives the right to seek damages or to assert any claims against the builder or the builder's employees, except as may be provided in this warranty agreement.

_____
(buyer's initials)

7. DISPUTE RESOLUTION: MEDIATION FIRST, THEN BINDING ARBITRATION

A. Mediation

Any controversy arising out of the condition of the home or the interpretation of this warranty, including, but not limited to, what constitutes a defect, any claim for damages against the builder, or any claim of negligence, fraud, breach of express warranty, breach of implied warranty, consumer protection act violations, and breach of contract, shall be decided by alternative dispute resolution. The parties agree to initially mediate in good faith and to attempt to achieve resolution of any dispute.

B. Binding Arbitration

In the event that the dispute is not fully resolved in mediation, the dispute shall then be submitted to binding arbitration. Arbitration shall be conducted in accordance with the Construction Industry Rules of the American Arbitration Association (see Resources) that are in effect at the time of the dispute. The arbitrator shall employ the standards of construction contained in the current edition of the Residential Construction Performance Guidelines (see Resources) in determining what constitutes a defect in construction. Should any party refuse or neglect to appear or to participate in arbitration proceedings, the arbitrator is empowered to decide the controversy in accordance with whatever evidence is presented. The arbitrator shall be authorized to order replacement or repair or to award damages. However, awarded damages shall not exceed the cost of replacement and repair. Each party shall be responsible for their own legal expenses and the cost of any expert witnesses. The fee for mediation and/or arbitration services shall be divided equally between the builder and the buyer.

_____   _____
(buyer's initials)   (builder's initials)

(*continued*)

FIGURE 4.2

Sample Builder's Limited Warranty Agreement
(Excluding Items Covered by the Magnuson-Moss Act)
(*Continued*)

I acknowledge having read, understood, and received a copy of this limited warranty agreement.

_____	_____
(buyer)	(builder)

Date _____

By _____

Title _____

Date _____

FIGURE 4.3

Sample Remodeler's Limited Warranty Agreement
for a Substantial Addition (Excluding Items Covered
by the Magnuson-Moss Act) (*Continued*)

Note: Building materials for substantial additions are not considered consumer products.

This limited warranty agreement is extended by _____
(the remodeler), whose address is _____,
to the owner _____ (the owner) of the residential property located
at the following address:
_____
_____
_____

This limited warranty excludes consequential damages, limits the duration of implied warranties, and provides for liquidated damages.

1. WHAT IS COVERED BY THE WARRANTY

The remodeler warrants that all construction related to the improvements made under the parties' contract substantially conforms to the plans and specifications and change orders for this job.

(continued)

FIGURE 4.3

**Sample Remodeler's Limited Warranty Agreement
for a Substantial Addition (Excluding Items Covered
by the Magnuson-Moss Act) (*Continued*)**

Description of improvements:

_____
_____
_____
_____

The owner acknowledges and agrees that these described improvements constitute a substantial addition to the realty under the definition set out in the Magnuson-Moss Warranty Act.

_____
(owner's initials)

The remodeler warrants that during the first thirty (30) days following substantial completion, the remodeler, after inspection of the property, will adjust or correct observable defects, or omissions.

Within one (1) year from the date of substantial completion, or commencement of use by the owner, whichever is first, the remodeler will repair or replace, at the remodeler's option, any latent defects, not apparent or ascertainable at the time of substantial completion or initial use, in the building materials or workmanship as defined by the standards of construction set out in the current edition of Residential Construction Performance Guidelines (see Resources). The owner agrees to accept reasonable matches in any repair or replacement in the event the specified or originally used item is no longer available.

2. WHAT IS NOT COVERED

This limited warranty does not cover the following items:

A. Damage resulting from fires, floods, storms, electrical malfunctions, accidents, or acts of God.
B. Damage from alterations, misuse, or abuse of the covered items by any person.
C. Damage resulting from the homeowner's failure to perform reasonable home maintenance.
D. Damage resulting from the owner's failure to observe any operating instructions furnished by the builder at the time of installation.
E. Damage resulting from a malfunction of equipment or lines of the telephone, gas, power, or water companies.
F. Any items listed as non-warrantable conditions on the list that is incorporated into this contract. The owner acknowledges receipt of the statement of nonwarrantable conditions. _____
(owner's initials)

(continued)

FIGURE 4.3

Sample Remodeler's Limited Warranty Agreement for a Substantial Addition (Excluding Items Covered by the Magnuson-Moss Act) (*Continued*)

G. Any item furnished or installed by the owner.

H. Any appliance, piece of equipment, or other item that is a consumer product for the purposes of the Magnuson-Moss Warranty Act, 15 United States Code §§ 2301 *et seq.*, installed or included in the owner's property. Examples of consumer products include, but are not limited to, dishwasher, garbage disposal, gas or electric range, range hood, refrigerator, microwave oven, trash compactor, garage door opener, washer, dryer, water heater, furnace, or heat pump. The only warranties for any appliance, pieces of equipment, or other item considered to be a consumer product for the purposes of the Magnuson Moss Act are those provided by the products' manufacturers.

3. MANUFACTURERS' WARRANTY

A. The remodeler has made any such manufacturers' warranties available to the owner for inspection, and the owner acknowledges receipt of these warranties, as requested.

_____
(owner's initials)

B. The remodeler hereby assigns (to the extent that they are assignable) and conveys to the owner all warranties provided to the remodeler on any manufactured items that have been installed or included in the owner's property. The owner accepts this assignment and acknowledges that the remodeler's only responsibility relating to such items is to lend assistance to the owner in settling any claim resulting from the installation of these products.

_____   _____
(owner's initials)   (remodeler's initials)

4. REMEDIES AND LIMITATIONS

A. The owner understands that the sole remedies under this limited warranty agreement are repair and replacement as set forth here. _____
(owner's initials)

B. With respect to any future claim whatsoever that may be asserted by the owner against the remodeler, the owner understands that the owner will have no right to recover or request compensation for, and the remodeler shall not be liable for, any of the following:
(1) Incidental, consequential, secondary, or punitive damages
(2) Damages for aggravation, mental anguish, emotional distress, or pain and suffering
(3) Attorney's fees or costs _____
(owner's initials)

C. Notwithstanding the provisions of this limited warranty agreement, if any liability arises on the part of the remodeler, the remodeler will pay the amount of actual provable damages arising from such liability, but the amount shall not exceed $_____. This amount, fixed

(*continued*)

FIGURE **4.3**

Sample Remodeler's Limited Warranty Agreement for a Substantial Addition (Excluding Items Covered by the Magnuson-Moss Act) (*Continued*)

as liquidated damages and not as a penalty, shall be the remodeler's complete and exclusive amount of liability. The provisions of this paragraph apply if loss or damage results directly or indirectly to persons or property from the performance of, or failure to perform, obligations imposed by the construction contract or from negligence, active or otherwise, of the remodeler or the remodeler's agents or employees.

The owner (a) understands that this provision limits the damages for which the remodeler will be liable and (b) acknowledges acceptance of this liquidated damages provision in consideration for the limited warranties provided by the remodeler and the other provisions of the construction contract. Therefore, the owner agrees to these liquidated damages clause if, notwithstanding the provisions of this limited warranty, liability should arise on the part of the remodeler. _____

(owner's initials)

D. **The remodeler hereby limits the duration of all implied warranties, including the implied warranties of merchantability, and fitness for a particular purpose, to one (1) year from the date of sale or the date of occupancy, whichever comes first. The owner specifically agrees to this limitation.**

_____
(owner's initials)

[Alternative to 4D]

[D. **The owner understands and agrees that no implied warranties whatsoever apply to improvement to the realty or to the components of the improvement. The remodeler disclaims, and the owner waives, any implied warranties, including, but not limited to, the implied warranty of merchantability and the implied warranty of fitness for a particular purpose.]**

E. This warranty is personal to the original owner and does not run with the property. The original owner may not assign, transfer, or convey this warranty without the prior written consent of the remodeler. _____

(owner's initials)

5. How to Obtain Service

If a problem develops during the warranty period, the owner must notify the remodeler of the specific problem in writing delivered to the remodeler at the address specified herein. This written statement of the problem must include the owner's name, address, telephone number, e-mail address, and a description of the nature of the problem. Within a reasonable time of receipt, the remodeler will inspect to determine if the problem is covered under this warranty.

(continued)

FIGURE 4.3

Sample Remodeler's Limited Warranty Agreement for a Substantial Addition (Excluding Items Covered by the Magnuson-Moss Act) (*Continued*)

If covered, the remodeler will perform the repair or replacement obligations under this warranty within a reasonable time and will diligently pursue this obligation. Repair work will be done during the remodeler's normal working hours, except in emergency situations where delay may cause additional damage. The owner agrees to provide the remodeler or remodeler's representative access to the house for all inspections and repairs. The owner also agrees to be present or to have a responsible adult present with authority to authorize the repair and to sign an acceptance-of-repair ticket upon completion.

6. WHERE TO GET HELP

For information concerning this warranty, the owner should contact the remodeler's customer service representative at

_____

(name, address, phone number, fax number, e-mail address)

Any notice or other document required or permitted to be delivered under this warranty, including written statements of problems, may be sent by first class mail to these authorized individuals at their addresses listed below.

_____   _____

(Name)   (Address)

_____   _____

(Name)   (Address)

7. THE ONLY WARRANTY GIVEN BY THE REMODELER—EXCLUSIVE REMEDY

(a) The owner has thoroughly examined the improvements to the realty; (b) the owner has received, has read, and understands this limited warranty; and (c) neither the remodeler nor the remodeler's representatives have made any guarantees, warranties, understandings, or representations that are not set forth in this document. This warranty document constitutes the exclusive remedy of all claims by the owner against the remodeler or the remodeler's employees. The owner specifically waives the right to seek damages or to assert any claims against the remodeler or the remodeler's employees, except as is provided in this warranty agreement.

8. DISPUTE RESOLUTION: MEDIATION FIRST, THEN BINDING ARBITRATION

A. Mediation

Any controversy arising out of the condition of the improvement to the realty or the interpretation of this warranty, including, but not limited to, what constitutes a defect, any claim for damages against the remodeler or any claim of negligence, fraud, breach of

(continued)

FIGURE 4.3

Sample Remodeler's Limited Warranty Agreement for a Substantial Addition (Excluding Items Covered by the Magnuson-Moss Act) (*Continued*)

express warranty, breach of implied warranty, consumer protection act violations, and breach of contract shall be decided by alternative dispute resolution. The parties agree to initially mediate in good faith and to attempt to achieve resolution of any dispute.

B. Binding Arbitration

In the event that the dispute is not fully resolved in mediation, the remodeler and the owner shall then submit the dispute to binding arbitration. The Arbitration shall be conducted in accordance with the Construction Industry Rules of the American Arbitration Association (see Resources) that are in effect at the time of the dispute. The arbitrator shall employ the construction guidelines contained in the current edition of the Residential Construction Performance Guidelines (see Resources) in determining what constitutes a defect in construction. Should any party refuse or neglect to appear or to participate in arbitration proceedings, the arbitrator is empowered to decide the controversy in accordance with whatever evidence is presented. The arbitrator shall be authorized to order replacement or repair or to award damages but awarded damages shall not exceed the cost of replacement and repair. Each party shall be responsible for its own legal expenses and the cost of any expert witnesses. The fee for mediation and/or arbitration services shall be divided equally between the remodeler and the owner.

_____   _____
(owner's initials)   (remodeler's initials)

I acknowledge having read, understood, and received a copy of this limited warranty agreement.

_____   _____
(Owner)   (Remodeler)

Date _____   By _____

Title _____

Date _____

FIGURE 4.4

Sample Statement of Nonwarrantable Conditions and Maintenance Obligations

This statement explains the conditions that are not subject to the builder's or remodeler's warranty. It also explains the home buyer's or owner's obligation to perform maintenance. Houses require more maintenance and care than most other products because they are constructed of hundreds of thousands of different components, each with its own special characteristics.

The buyer or owner understands that, like every product made by human hand, a house or a home improvement is not usually 100 percent perfect. This fact is true with new cars, and it is true for homes. Some minor flaw or unforeseeable defect could require adjustment or touching up. The builder or remodeler will correct certain defects that arise during defined time periods after construction has been completed, as is described in the limited warranty provided to you. This statement of nonwarrantable conditions is a part of that warranty. In addition, some items that are not covered by the builder's or remodeler's warranty may be covered by separate manufacturers' warranties.

Home buyers or owners should read this statement carefully to understand what the builder or remodeler has not agreed to correct. This document will alert the buyer or owner to matters of maintenance that (a) are the responsibility of the buyer or owner and (b) could lead to problems if neglected or not performed.

The following list outlines some of the conditions that are not warranted by the builder or remodeler. **Note:** This list is not exclusive, and the builder or remodeler may add to it. Of the items listed and discussed below, remodelers may want to include only those that pertain to a particular job because many of these listed items will not apply to every job.

1. CONCRETE

Concrete foundations, steps, walks, drives, and patios can develop minor cracks that do not affect the structural integrity of the building. These cracks are caused by characteristics of the concrete itself. No reasonable method of eliminating these cracks exists. This condition does not affect the strength of the building. For more information on the guidelines for determining whether cracks of any type should be repaired, consult Residential Construction Performance Guidelines (see Resources).

2. MASONRY AND MORTAR

Masonry and mortar can develop minor cracks from shrinkage of either the mortar or the brick. This condition is normal and should not be considered a defect.

3. WOOD

Wood will sometimes check or crack or the fibers will spread apart because of the drying-out process. This condition is most often caused by the heat inside the house or by exposure to the sun on the outside of the house. This condition is considered normal, and the homeowner is responsible for any maintenance or repairs resulting from it.

(continued)

FIGURE **4.4**

Sample Statement of Nonwarrantable Conditions and Maintenance Obligations (*Continued*)

4. SHEETROCK AND DRYWALL

Sheetrock or drywall will sometimes develop nail pops or settlement cracks, which are a normal part of the drying-out process. A nail pop occurs when wood shrinks and pushes a nail part way out of the wood. These items can easily be handled by the homeowner with spackling during normal redecorating. If the homeowner wishes, however, the builder or remodeler will send a worker at the end of the one (1) year warranty period to make the necessary repairs. These repairs will not include repainting.

5. FLOOR SQUEAKS

Floor squeaks may appear and disappear over time with changes in the weather and humidity. Technical experts generally conclude that little can be done about floor squeaks, and the condition is not considered to be a defect.

6. FLOORS

Floors are not warranted for damage caused by neglect or the incidents of use. Wood, tile, and carpet all require maintenance. Floor casters are recommended to prevent scratching or chipping of wood or tile, and stains should be promptly cleaned from carpets, wood, or tile to prevent discoloration. Carpet tends to loosen in damp weather and will stretch tight again in dry weather.

7. CAULK

Exterior and interior caulking, including caulking around bathtubs, shower stalls, and ceramic tile surfaces, may crack or bleed somewhat in the months after installation. These conditions are normal and should not be considered a problem. The maintenance or replacement of interior or exterior caulk is the homeowner's responsibility.

8. DISCOLORED BRICKS

Bricks may discolor because of rain run-off, weathering by wind, or bleaching by the sun. Efflorescence—the formation of salts on the surface of brick walls—is a common occurrence. It results from a brick's normal absorption of moisture. Efflorescence can be removed by cleaning, and this task is the homeowner's responsibility.

9. BROKEN GLASS

The replacement of any window glass or mirrors that are broken after the final inspection is the responsibility of the homeowner.

(continued)

FIGURE 4.4

Sample Statement of Nonwarrantable Conditions and Maintenance Obligations (*Continued*)

10. FROZEN PIPES

The homeowner must take precautions to prevent freezing of pipes and sillcocks during extremely cold weather. These precautions may include removing outside hoses from sillcocks, keeping the house adequately heated, leaving faucets slightly open to drip, or turning off the water supply if the house is to be unoccupied for an extended period during cold weather.

11. STAINED WOOD

Stained materials will normally display a variation of colors because of the different textures and grains of wood. Because of changes in humidity, doors with panels may at times dry out and leave a small space of bare wood. This exposed wood should not be considered a defect. The bare wood can be easily touched up, and it is the homeowner's responsibility to do so.

12. PAINT

Good-quality paint has been used internally and externally on this home. Nevertheless, exterior paint can sometimes crack or check. The reason is often something other than the quality of the paint. You should avoid such practices as:

- Directing lawn sprinkler spray onto painted areas.
- Scrubbing interior latex-painted walls because scrubbing may remove the paint.
- Striking or rubbing furniture against painted walls.

The best paint can chip or stain if it is not cared for properly. Any painting deficiencies that occur after occupancy or that are not noted at final inspection are the homeowner's responsibility. Please note that all paint will fade and deteriorate over time, and you will be required to repaint periodically.

13. COSMETIC ITEMS

The builder or remodeler is not responsible for ordinary wear and tear, for effects of weather, nor for the acts of the homeowner or third parties that may mar, stain, or otherwise damage the features of the home. Chips, scratches, or marks in tile, woodwork, walls, porcelain, brick, mirrors, plumbing fixtures, marble and solid surface countertops, lighting fixtures, kitchen and other appliances, vinyl floors, cabinets, and other features that are not noted at the final inspection are nonwarrantable conditions. The upkeep of all cosmetic appearances of the house is solely the homeowner's responsibility.

(continued)

FIGURE 4.4

Sample Statement of Nonwarrantable Conditions and Maintenance Obligations (*Continued*)

14. PLUMBING

Adjustments for dripping faucets, sink, bath and toilet fixtures, and toilet seats are covered by the builder's or remodeler's warranty for a thirty-day (30) period only. After that period, they are the homeowner's responsibility. Stoppages from hair clogs, toilet tissue, or foreign materials in pipes and drains are the responsibility of the homeowner. If the builder or remodeler is called upon to service the plumbing during the warranty period, and the service person determines that the problem is the result of foreign materials in the line, the homeowner will be billed for the service call.

15. ALTERATIONS TO GRADING

The homeowner's lot has been graded to ensure proper drainage away from the home's foundation. Should the homeowner want to change the drainage pattern for landscaping, for the installation of patio or service walks, or for any other reason, the homeowner should be sure to retain a proper drainage slope. The builder or remodeler shall not be responsible for any drainage problems if the established drainage pattern is subsequently altered.

16. LAWN AND SHRUBS

The builder or remodeler accepts no responsibility for the growth of grass or shrubs. Once the yard has been graded, seeded (and/or sod installed), and fertilized, the homeowner bears the responsibility for watering, fertilizing, and feeding all plants and grass sufficiently and for planting additional ground cover where necessary to prevent erosion. The builder will not regrade a yard or remove or replace any shrubs or trees, except for those that may be noted as dead or diseased at the final inspection.

17. ROOF

During the first year of occupancy or the first year following installation, the builder's or remodeler's warranty covers workmanship and materials. The builder or remodeler is not responsible for any damage done by the homeowner or third parties caused by walking on the roof for any reason, including but not limited to installation of a satellite dish or a television antenna. After that one-year period has expired, the warranty on the roof is a manufacturer's warranty for material only, and it is prorated over the period designated in the manufacturer's warranty. Warranty claims for any defects in roofing materials must be made to the manufacturer in accordance with the manufacturer's warranty procedures.

18. HEATING AND AIR-CONDITIONING

The furnace, heat pump, and other heating and air-conditioning equipment are covered by a manufacturer's warranty and not by the builder's or remodeler's warranty. The homeowner is

(continued)

FIGURE 4.4

Sample Statement of Nonwarrantable Conditions and Maintenance Obligations (*Continued*)

responsible for keeping the filters clean and changing them in accordance with the manufacturer's recommendations. A failure to do so may void the manufacturer's warranty. Periodic checking and servicing of heating and air-conditioning equipment in accordance with the manufacturer's recommendations will help prevent problems, and they are the responsibility of the homeowner.

19. INDOOR AIR QUALITY

Radon Notice. Radon is a radioactive, colorless, and odorless gas that has been found in homes throughout the United States. It is the second leading cause of lung cancer (next to smoking). The gas occurs naturally in soil and may enter a home through cracks or holes in the foundation or through water supplied by wells. If you are building or buying a new home or planning any major structural renovation, such as converting an unfinished basement area into living space, test the lower levels of the home for radon. If your test results indicate a radon problem, radon-resistant techniques can be inexpensively included as part of the construction or the renovation process. Because major renovations can change the level of radon in any home, always test again after the renovation work is completed.

The homeowner has been furnished with a copy of A Citizen's Guide to Radon: The Guide to Protecting Yourself and Your Family. (See Resources).

I have received, read, and understand this statement of non-warrantable items and homeowner maintenance obligations. I understand that these non-warrantable items have not been contracted for, and I agree not to hold the builder or remodeler liable thereon.

_____   _____
(buyer or owner)   (builder or remodeler)

Date _____   By _____

                                        Title _____

                                        Date _____

CHAPTER 5

CLAIMS PROCEDURES

Have established procedures in place to respond to warranty claims from your customers. These procedures ensure that any claim process goes smoothly and that you and your homeowner know what to expect throughout the process. Responding to warranty claims is vitally important because any non-performance of your warranty obligations will have far-reaching implications, not the least of which could be costly litigation and damage to your professional reputation.

Operating a customer-oriented business such as home building or remodeling requires builders and remodelers to be forward thinkers. Inevitably, you will encounter customers who are unsatisfied with certain aspects of a project you complete for them. To reduce the number of potential warranty claims on new projects or to control your repair costs on existing ones, consider implementing various risk-management procedures into your daily operations. By implementing some basic steps up front and consistently following them, you can reduce potential problems later:

Responding to warranty claims is vitally important—any non-performance of your warranty obligations will have far-reaching implications.

- Be proactive in completing your project. Do not promise more than you intend to do and complete the project in a timely fashion.
- Implement *best practices* for responding to claims and conducting any necessary repairs.
- Adopt and use uniform construction guidelines on your projects and tell the customer about those guidelines.

Be Proactive in Approaching Your Building Project

One of the best ways to minimize claims is to adopt proactive procedures in building and completing your projects. You can minimize claims up front by conducting frequent inspections on work as the job progresses and at the end of each phase of completion.

For example, inspect trade contractors' work on your jobsite on a regular basis. Keep a list of any items that need fixing and correct them or have them fixed right away. Ensure trade contractors fix any problems you identify by the time they complete their portion of the job and before they leave the jobsite. That way, you do not have to wait for them to return before you can move to the next construction phase. Frequent inspections allow you to identify and correct any problems immediately instead of after-the-fact.

Correcting problems as they occur should also minimize or eliminate potential claims after completion of the construction project. If you adopt uniform procedures for inspecting work progress, make repairs as they occur, and maintain records of items you repair, you should be able to complete your projects in a timely fashion. These procedures can help you identify problems before they become a problem for your customer and, ultimately, a claim against you.

If you receive a claim, proactively respond to the customer as you do during the initial project. Conduct frequent inspections to ensure your employees complete the work to your standards and document procedures taken during the repair. Keep your customers informed on the progress of the repair and provide them with a copy of any paperwork prepared in response to the claim.

Establish and Implement Best Practices

As builders and remodelers, your business should develop and implement *best practices* that detail how you and your company will respond to warranty claims made by homeowners. With such procedures in place, all parties will know what to expect should a claim arise. Establish and maintain clear and consistent business practices so that you, your employees, and your homeowners know the procedures and steps to resolve claims. Have specific procedures for receiving, responding to, and addressing claims. Develop uniform procedures for all claims, regardless of whether the particular claim is small or large. Following standard procedures ensures that your company responds consistently to all claims and resolves them in a timely manner. Such procedures set the stage for happy customers and repeat and referral business.

Consider incorporating your procedures into your contract. Whether you include procedures in the contract or keep them separate, make your procedures easy to understand. Confusing procedures could leave some customers unsure if you want to address their claims or could lead them to believe you are unable, unwilling, or incapable of correcting the claim to their satisfaction.

Confusing procedures could leave some customers unsure whether you legitimately want to address their claims.

As part of your procedures, specify warranty work or other claims are performed during regular business hours. Your procedures should also establish a repair time or schedule rather than having your employees make random trips to the site as a claim arises. For example, you may adopt a procedure for two or three scheduled visits—30 to 90 days after settlement and another visit shortly before the end of the first year. The last visit should be to respond to and wrap up any outstanding claims. If you establish a schedule to complete work under a claim, follow it and complete the repair when promised.

Consider training one or two employees to specifically respond to customer claims as your warranty claims person(s). You should not send anyone who is available because this practice could lead to inconsistent procedures or uneven results. In addition, consider developing a checklist for documenting claims so that you can readily identify any claims and note any corrective action needed or taken. Be sure this checklist is clear, concise, and has space to document necessary information. The form should contain space to:

- Describe the claim.
- Allow your employee to note corrective action or explain why there was not a repair.
- Include your employee's name and the dates they went to the site.
- Have the homeowner date and initial the form indicating that your employee came to the site and if there was a repair.

Use this checklist for all warranty claims so your claims employee knows the established procedures. Furthermore, be sure your claims employee fills out the form completely. Consider using a self-duplicating form so your employee can easily give the homeowner a copy for their records before leaving the site and to retain a copy with your other documents for that project. Consistency and uniformity are key when responding to warranty claims.

Construction Performance Guidelines

When responding to claims, do not promise too much only to fail to deliver. As part of your best-practices procedures, consider using construction performance guidelines or building codes such as the International

Residential Code and incorporating these directly into your original contract with a new customer or homeowner. Utilizing uniform guidelines notifies your homeowner and others involved in the project the guidelines you intend to follow and what they can expect. Incorporating such guidelines into your contract provides your customers with notice of construction tolerances should a customer make a claim for repairs based on defective workmanship or materials.

For example, the National Association of Home Builders (NAHB) publishes *Residential Construction Performance Guidelines for Professional Builders & Remodelers*. If you incorporate these guidelines in your contract, it is a benchmark your company will strive to meet or exceed in the original construction and any warranty repair.

NAHB publishes a consumer version of these guidelines that you can provide to your customers for reference. As any questions come up, the customer can turn to the guidelines for reference and information. This procedure allows the customer to know at the start of the project the acceptable construction tolerances in the given area, whether they involve concrete, stain, tile, or other aspects. Using performance guidelines also lends professionalism and credibility to your work.

CHAPTER 6

NOTICE AND OPPORTUNITY TO REPAIR (NOR) LEGISLATION

Throughout the country, building professionals are experiencing increased construction-defect litigation, lawsuits, and general liability insurance costs. Easy access to courts by potential litigants means that builders, remodelers and homeowners often end up in time-consuming and expensive litigation as their primary means for remedying construction-related problems. The increase in construction-defect cases litigated also means that homeowners and home builders will see much higher costs for housing generally.

Widespread construction-defect litigation has also created a liability insurance crisis for the entire building industry. Builders, remodelers, and developers are experiencing more difficulty in obtaining general liability insurance coverage. Moreover, available liability insurance coverage is now much more expensive and restrictive.

NOR legislation arose as a means of addressing these issues. By providing building professionals and homeowners with alternative methods to solve problems and complaints, NOR legislation addresses construction defects in a positive and fair manner. Designed to encourage prelitigation resolution of claims for construction defects, NOR provisions offer fairness, a measure of predictability and speed to the process of resolving construction defect disputes. Currently, just over half of the states have adopted NOR legislation.

Common Components of NOR Legislation

Typically, in states that have NOR legislation, statutes require that homeowners notify the builder or remodeler of a claim before filing a lawsuit. NOR statutes also give the builder an opportunity to inspect the site, allow them to repair the defect, or pay money in lieu of repairing the defect. NOR statutes also require that notice be made in writing and done within a certain period following discovery of the defect. Notice periods can range anywhere from 90 days to 18 months, depending on individual state statutory requirements. Most statutes that identify a time frame also require the builder or remodeler to respond in some fashion by making a request to inspect the alleged defects, offering to repair the alleged defect, making an offer to settle the claim by payment, or disputing the claim.

If the builder responds by offering to repair the defect, repairs must generally start by a certain date, unless the parties can agree on another time for the repairs to occur. For example, Colorado allows the claimant and the builder to alter the procedure for the notice of claim set out in the statute as long as the claimant has already sent the notice of claim. Col. Rev. Stat. § 13-20-803.5(8). If the builder rejects the homeowner's claim and does not remedy or settle the claim, the homeowner may file suit against the builder without further notice. In addition, some states allow the owner to reject a proposed repair offer.

If you conduct business in a state that has adopted NOR legislation, you must become familiar with the requirements of the particular sections of the statute. Figure 6.1 is a list of states with current or pending NOR legislation.

Pay particular attention to any statute sections that require you to give preliminary notice to the homeowner, in either the contract for sale or at closing, as well as any time limitations or requirements. Some states require builders to give notice of NOR legislation in the initial sales contract or as part of the closing documents. Such notice may require the contract or closing documents use specific statutory language, typeface, font size and/or place the notice in a stated section of the documents to comply with the statute. Figure 6.2 is a list of states that require mandatory notice provision.

Some states require notice of NOR legislation in the initia lsales contract or in closing documents . . . and may require statutory language, typeface, or location.

The statute sections discussed in this chapter do not necessarily represent every state that may have NOR legislation or statutes with language similar to NOR. Check if your state has NOR legislation or similar provisions for notice and opportunity to repair. Most states include links to statutes and regulations on their state web pages; check for updates by going directly to your state's site.

States Without NOR Legislation

As discussed, about half of the states have a type of notice provision and specific NOR legislation. If you conduct business in a state that does not have legislation, you can add a provision to your contract in

FIGURE 6.1

States with Current Notice and Opportunity to Repair Laws

State	Statute Section
Alaska*	§§ 09.45.881–900
Arizona	§ 12-1361–1365
California	Civil Code §§ 895–945.5
Colorado	§§ 13-20-801–13-20-807
Florida*	§§ 558.001–558.005
Georgia*	§§ 8-2-35–43
Hawaii*	Haw. Rev. Stat. § 672E-1–13
Idaho	§§ 6-2501–6-2504
Indiana*	§ 32-27-3
Iowa***	§§ 686.1–686.7
Kansas*	§ 60-4701–4710
Kentucky*	§ 411.250-266
Louisiana**	§§ 9:3142–9:3150
Michigan	§§ 339.2411—contractor license complaints only
Minnesota	§ 327A.02, subd. 5
Mississippi**	§§ 83-58-7
Missouri	Mo. Rev. Stat. §§ 436.350–365
Montana	§ 70-19-426–428
Nevada	§§ 40.600–770
New Hampshire*	N.H. Rev. Stat. § 359-G:1–8
New York	N.Y. General Business Law § 777-A (4)(a)
North Dakota	N.D. Cent. Code § 43-07-26
Ohio*	§ 1312.03
Oklahoma*	15 Okl. St. Ann. § 765.5–6
Oregon*	O.R.S. §§ 701.560–701.600
South Carolina	S.C. Code Ann. § 40-59-810
South Dakota	S.D. Codified Laws § 21-1-15-16
Tennessee	Tenn. Code. Ann. § 66-36-101-103
Texas*	Tx. Prop. Code §§ 27.001-27.007
Virginia	Va. Code § 55.1-357
Washington*	Wash. Rev. Code §§ 64.50.005–64.50.060
West Virginia*	W. Va. Code §§ 21-11A-1–21-11A-17
Wisconsin	Wis. Stat. § 895.07

* These statutes require builders to include mandatory notice or contract provisions either at the time of contracting with an owner or in the contract itself and may require that such provisions substantially comply with language provided in the statute, and they must be conspicuous.

** These statutes require notice of statutory provisions at closing but do not require use of mandatory language.

*** These statutes only apply to class actions.

FIGURE **6.2**

States That Require Mandatory Notice Provisions

Mandatory Provisions

Alaska
§ 09.45.893(c)
Requires that notice be given in substantially the format that appears in the adjoining column.

ALASKA LAW AT AS 09.45.881 - 09.45.899 CONTAINS IMPORTANT REQUIREMENTS THAT YOU MUST FOLLOW BEFORE YOU MAY FILE A COURT ACTION FOR DEFECTIVE DESIGN, CONSTRUCTION, OR REMODELING AGAINST THE DESIGNER, BUILDER, OR REMODELER OF YOUR HOME. WITHIN ONE YEAR OF THE DISCOVERY OF A DESIGN, CONSTRUCTION, OR REMODELING DEFECT, BEFORE YOU FILE A COURT ACTION, YOU MUST DELIVER TO THE DESIGNER, BUILDER, OR REMODELER A WRITTEN NOTICE OF ANY DESIGN, CONSTRUCTION, OR REMODELING CONDITIONS YOU ALLEGE ARE DEFECTIVE IN ORDER TO PROVIDE YOUR DESIGNER, BUILDER, OR REMODELER WITH THE OPPORTUNITY TO MAKE AN OFFER TO REPAIR OR PAY FOR THE DEFECTS. YOU ARE NOT OBLIGATED TO ACCEPT ANY OFFER MADE BY THE DESIGNER, BUILDER, OR REMODELER. THERE ARE STRICT DEADLINES AND PROCEDURES UNDER STATE LAW, AND FAILURE TO FOLLOW THEM MAY AFFECT YOUR RIGHT TO FILE A COURT ACTION. ALASKA LAW AT AS 09.45.895 CONTAINS LIMITATIONS TO THE AMOUNT OF DAMAGES THAT MAY BE RECOVERED IN A COURT ACTION FOR DEFECTIVE DESIGN, CONSTRUCTION, OR REMODELING.

Arizona
§ 32-1155 (A)-(C)
Requires the original contract to contain the language in the next column, or provide separate notice of the following, and be prominently displayed, in at least 10-point bold type, and initialed by the buyer.

Under Arizona Revised Statutes § 32-1155, a buyer of a dwelling has the right to file a written complaint against the homebuilder with the Arizona registrar of contractors within two years after the close of escrow or actual occupancy, whichever occurs first, for the commission of an act in violation of Arizona Revised Statutes § 32-1154, subsection A.

California

California requires the builder to record on the title a notice of the existence of the document disclosure procedures in § 910 and include with the original sales documents and further requires that the purchaser and builder's sales representative initial and acknowledge receipt of Civil Code §§ 910 – 938. *See* Cal. Civ. Code § 910(f) and (g).

(continued)

46

FIGURE 6.2

States That Require Mandatory Notice Provisions (*Continued*)

Mandatory Provisions

Florida

§ 558.005(6) states that the following applies to any written contract for improvement of real property after October 1, 2009.

CHAPTER 558 NOTICE OF CLAIM

ANY CLAIMS FOR CONSTRUCTION DEFECTS ARE SUBJECT TO THE NOTICE AND CURE PROVISIONS OF CHAPTER 558, FLORIDA STATUTES.

Georgia

§ 8-2-41(b) requires that notice be given in substantially the format that appears in the adjoining column.

GEORGIA LAW CONTAINS IMPORTANT REQUIREMENTS YOU MUST FOLLOW BEFORE YOU MAY FILE A LAWSUIT OR OTHER ACTION FOR DEFECTIVE CONSTRUCTION AGAINST THE CONTRACTOR WHO CONSTRUCTED, IMPROVED, OR REPAIRED YOUR HOME. NINETY DAYS BEFORE YOU FILE YOUR LAWSUIT OR OTHER ACTION, YOU MUST SERVE ON THE CONTRACTOR A WRITTEN NOTICE OF ANY CONSTRUCTION CONDITIONS YOU ALLEGE ARE DEFECTIVE. UNDER THE LAW, A CONTRACTOR HAS THE OPPORTUNITY TO MAKE AN OFFER TO REPAIR OR PAY FOR THE DEFECTS OR BOTH. YOU ARE NOT OBLIGATED TO ACCEPT ANY OFFER MADE BY A CONTRACTOR. THERE ARE STRICT DEADLINES AND PROCEDURES UNDER STATE LAW, AND FAILURE TO FOLLOW THEM MAY AFFECT YOUR ABILITY TO FILE A LAWSUIT OR OTHER ACTION.

Hawaii

§ 672E-11(a) - (b) requires notice be conspicuous and included as part of the contract, shall explicitly reference this chapter, and shall be in substantially the following form: (See adjoining column).

CHAPTER 672E OF THE HAWAII REVISED STATUTES CONTAINS IMPORTANT REQUIREMENTS YOU MUST FOLLOW BEFORE YOU MAY FILE A LAWSUIT OR OTHER ACTION FOR DEFECTIVE CONSTRUCTION AGAINST THE CONTRACTOR WHO DESIGNED, REPAIRED, OR CONSTRUCTED YOUR HOME OR FACILITY. NINETY DAYS BEFORE YOU FILE YOUR LAWSUIT OR OTHER ACTION, YOU MUST SERVE ON THE CONTRACTOR A WRITTEN NOTICE OF ANY CONSTRUCTION CONDITIONS YOU ALLEGE ARE DEFECTIVE. UNDER THE LAW, A CONTRACTOR HAS THE OPPORTUNITY TO MAKE AN OFFER TO REPAIR AND/OR PAY FOR THE DEFECTS. YOU ARE NOT OBLIGATED TO ACCEPT ANY OFFER MADE BY A CONTRACTOR. THERE ARE STRICT DEADLINES AND PROCEDURES UNDER THE LAW, AND FAILURE TO FOLLOW THEM MAY NEGATIVELY AFFECT YOUR ABILITY TO FILE A LAWSUIT OR OTHER ACTION.

(*continued*)

FIGURE **6.2**

States That Require Mandatory Notice Provisions (*Continued*)

Mandatory Provisions

Indiana
§ 32-27-3-12(a)-(b) requires notice must be provided to each homeowner of the right to cure and that notice must be conspicuous and included as part of the contract and shall be in substantially the following form: (See adjoining column).

IC 32-27-3 CONTAINS IMPORTANT REQUIREMENTS YOU MUST FOLLOW BEFORE YOU MAY FILE A LAWSUIT FOR DEFECTIVE CONSTRUCTION AGAINST THE CONTRACTOR OR BUILDER OF YOUR HOME. SIXTY (60) DAYS BEFORE YOU FILE YOUR LAWSUIT, YOU MUST DELIVER TO THE CONTRACTOR OR BUILDER A WRITTEN NOTICE OF ANY CONSTRUCTION CONDITIONS YOU ALLEGE ARE DEFECTIVE AND PROVIDE YOUR CONTRACTOR OR BUILDER THE OPPORTUNITY TO MAKE AN OFFER TO REPAIR OR PAY FOR THE DEFECTS. YOU ARE NOT OBLIGATED TO ACCEPT ANY OFFER MADE BY THE BUILDER OR CONTRACTOR. HOWEVER, IF YOU UNREASONABLY REJECT A REASONABLE WRITTEN OFFER AND COMMENCE AN ACTION AGAINST THE BUILDER OR CONTRACTOR, A COURT MAY AWARD ATTORNEY'S FEES AND COSTS TO THE BUILDER OR CONTRACTOR. THERE ARE STRICT DEADLINES AND PROCEDURES UNDER STATE LAW, AND FAILURE TO FOLLOW THEM MAY AFFECT YOUR ABILITY TO FILE A LAWSUIT.

Kansas
§ 6-4706(a)-(b) requires notice to be given and states that it may be included as part of the contract; such notice shall be conspicuous and be given in substantially the following form: (See adjoining column.)

Kansas law contains important requirements you must follow before you may file a lawsuit for defective construction against the contractor who constructed your home. Ninety days before you file your lawsuit, you must deliver to the contractor a written notice of any construction conditions you allege are defective and provide your contractor the opportunity to make an offer to repair or pay for the defects. You are not obligated to accept any offer made by the contractor. There are strict deadlines and procedures under state law, and failure to follow them may affect your ability to file a lawsuit.

Kentucky
§ 411.260(2) requires that notice be given in substantially the format that appears in the adjoining column.

SECTIONS 411.250 TO 411.260 OF THE KENTUCKY REVISED STATUTES CONTAIN IMPORTANT REQUIREMENTS YOU MUST FOLLOW BEFORE YOU MAY FILE A LAWSUIT FOR DEFECTIVE CONSTRUCTION AGAINST THE BUILDER OF YOUR HOME. YOU MUST DELIVER TO THE BUILDER A WRITTEN NOTICE OF ANY CONSTRUCTION CONDITIONS YOU ALLEGE ARE DEFECTIVE AND PROVIDE YOUR BUILDER THE OPPORTUNITY TO MAKE AN OFFER TO REPAIR OR PAY FOR THE DEFECTS. YOU ARE NOT OBLIGATED TO ACCEPT ANY OFFER MADE BY THE BUILDER. THERE ARE STRICT DEADLINES AND PROCEDURES UNDER STATE LAW, AND FAILURE TO FOLLOW THEM MAY AFFECT YOUR ABILITY TO FILE A LAWSUIT.

(*continued*)

FIGURE 6.2

States That Require Mandatory Notice Provisions (*Continued*)

Mandatory Provisions

Louisiana

Louisiana requires that the builder give the owner written notice of the requirements of this chapter at the time of closing, but does not specify specific language for the notice. See § 9:3145

Maine
Me. Rev. Stat. Ann. §1487(10.) The Maine Home Construction Contracts Act requires all contracts to build a residence to contain a warranty statement which reads: (See adjoining column.)

"In addition to any additional warranties agreed to by the parties, the contractor warrants that the work will be free from faulty materials; constructed according to the standards of the building code applicable for this location; constructed in a skillful manner and fit for habitation or appropriate use. The warranty rights and remedies set forth in the Maine Uniform Commercial Code apply to this contract."

Maryland
Real property Code § 10-605
This section requires builders who provide a statutory new home warranty to conspicuously include this notice in the contract in at least 12-point type: (See the adjoining column.)

"Notice to Purchaser"
"Your new home will be covered by a new home warranty that meets the minimum requirements established under Title 10, Subtitle 6 of the Real Property Article of the Annotated Code of Maryland. Before you sign this contract, your builder is required to give you a copy of the warranty coverage you will receive. "The name of the new home warranty security plan in which your builder is currently a participant is_____. You are strongly encouraged to call the new home warranty security plan at _____ to verify (i) that your builder is in good standing with this company, and (ii) that your new home will be covered by a warranty from this company. "If the builder is not a participant in good standing with this company on the date of this contract, or if the new home has not been registered in the plan on or before the warranty date, then it is a material breach of the contract and you are entitled to whatever remedies are provided by law, including, but not limited to, rescission or cancellation of this contract and, except in the case of a construction contract for a new home built on your own property, a refund of any money paid to the builder for your new home. "On the day that you first occupy the new home, settle on the new home, make the final payment to the builder on your new home, or obtain an occupancy permit for a new home if the new home is built on your own property, whichever is earlier, you will be provided with evidence that a new home warranty exists for your new home and that coverage begins on that date. You will be provided with a signed new home warranty within 60 days from the date the coverage begins.

(continued)

FIGURE 6.2

States That Require Mandatory Notice Provisions (*Continued*)

Mandatory Provisions

Maryland
(*continued*)

"The terms used in this notice shall have the same meanings as provided in Title 10, Subtitle 6 of the Real Property Article of the Annotated Code of Maryland."

Mississippi

Mississippi does not require builders to use specific language when notifying an owner of the notice requirements of this chapter. But the statute does require the builder to provide notice of the chapter requirements at the time of closing. "If the builder does not provide such notice, the warranties provided in this chapter shall be extended for a period of time equal to the time between the warranty commencement date and date notice was given." See § 83-58-7.

New Hampshire
a residence in which the contract amount exceeds $5,000, the contractor shall provide written notice to the owner of the residence of the contractor's right to resolve alleged construction defects before a home owner may commence litigation against the contractor. Such notice shall be conspicuous and may be included as part of the contract. The notice shall be in substantially the following form: (See adjoining column.)

NEW HAMPSHIRE LAW, RSA 359-G, CONTAINS IMPORTANT REQUIREMENTS YOU MUST FOLLOW BEFORE YOU MAY FILE A LAWSUIT OR OTHER ACTION FOR DEFECTIVE CONSTRUCTION AGAINST THE CONTRACTOR WHO CONSTRUCTED, REMODELED, OR REPAIRED YOUR HOME. SIXTY DAYS BEFORE YOU FILE YOUR LAWSUIT OR OTHER ACTION, YOU MUST SERVE ON THE CONTRACTOR A WRITTEN NOTICE OF ANY CONSTRUCTION CONDITIONS YOU ALLEGE ARE DEFECTIVE UNDER THE LAW. A CONTRACTOR HAS THE OPPORTUNITY TO MAKE AN OFFER TO REPAIR AND/OR PAY FOR THE DEFECTS. THERE ARE STRICT DEADLINES AND PROCEDURES UNDER STATE LAW, AND FAILURE TO FOLLOW THEM MAY AFFECT YOUR ABILITY TO FILE A LAWSUIT OR OTHER ACTION.

Ohio
§ 1312.03 requires notice to the owner upon entering into a contract; such notice may be included in

OHIO LAW CONTAINS IMPORTANT REQUIREMENTS YOU MUST FOLLOW BEFORE YOU MAY FILE A LAWSUIT OR COMMENCE ARBITRATION PROCEEDINGS FOR DEFECTIVE CONSTRUCTION AGAINST THE RESIDENTIAL CONTRACTOR WHO CONSTRUCTED YOUR HOME. AT LEAST SIXTY DAYS BEFORE YOU FILE A LAWSUIT OR COMMENCE ARBITRATION

(*continued*)

FIGURE

States That Require Mandatory Notice Provisions (*Continued*)

Mandatory Provisions

Ohio
(*continued*)
the contract itself,
or in a separate
document.

Notice must be
conspicuous and in
substantially
this form.

PROCEEDINGS, YOU MUST PROVIDE THE CONTRACTOR
WITH A WRITTEN NOTICE OF THE CONDITIONS YOU ALLEGE
ARE DEFECTIVE. UNDER CHAPTER 1312, OF THE OHIO
REVISED CODE, THE CONTRACTOR HAS AN OPPORTUNITY
TO OFFER TO REPAIR OR PAY FOR THE DEFECTS. YOU ARE
NOT OBLIGATED TO ACCEPT ANY OFFER THE CONTRACTOR
MAKES. THERE ARE STRICT DEADLINES AND PROCEDURES
UNDER STATE LAW, AND FAILURE TO FOLLOW THEM MAY
AFFECT YOUR ABILITY TO FILE A LAWSUIT OR COMMENCE
ARBITRATION PROCEEDINGS.

Oklahoma
15 Okl.St.Ann.
§ 765.6
Oklahoma NOR
protections are not
operative unless the
contract contains the
above provisions.

A contract for the construction of a new residence or for an altera-
tion of, repair of, or addition to an existing residence may include
provisions which: (See the adjoining column.)

1. Require a homeowner, prior to filing a lawsuit for construction
   defects, to present to the contractor a written notice of construction defects; and
2. Allows the contractor to inspect any construction defects and
   present to the homeowner a written response which shall include
   the contractor's offer to repair defects or compensate homeowner
   for such defects within thirty (30) days after receipt of the notice
   of defects.

If such provisions are included in a contract, the homeowner shall
not file a lawsuit against the contractor until the condition's precedent
have been fulfilled. In the event the homeowner files a lawsuit against
the contractor without fulfilling the conditions precedent, the contractor shall be entitled to a stay of proceedings until such conditions have
been fulfilled. If the conditions precedent has been fulfilled, the homeowner may seek remedies against the contractor as provided by law.

Texas
§ 27.007(a) requires
that a "written con-
tract subject to this
chapter must contain

This contract is subject to Chapter 27 of the Texas Property Code.
The provisions of that chapter may affect your right to recover
damages arising from the performance of this contract. If you have
a complaint concerning a construction defect arising from the performance of this contract and that defect has not been corrected

(*continued*)

FIGURE **6.2**

States That Require Mandatory Notice Provisions
(*Continued*)

Mandatory Provisions

Texas
(*continued*)
next to the signature
lines in the contract a
notice printed or typed
in 10-point boldface
type or the computer
equivalent that reads
substantially similar to
the text in theadjoining
column."

through normal warranty service, you must provide the notice
required by Chapter 27 of the Texas Property Code to the contractor
by certified mail, return receipt requested, not later than the 60th day
before the date you file suit to recover damages in a court of law or
initiate arbitration. The notice must refer to Chapter 27 of the Texas
Property Code and must describe the construction defect. If requested
by the contractor, you must provide the contractor an opportunity
to inspect and cure the defect as provided by Section 27.004 of the
Texas Property Code.

Washington
§ 64.50.050(2)
requires that notice
be given in substan-
tially the format that
appears in the adjoin-
ing column.

CHAPTER 64.50 RCW CONTAINS IMPORTANT REQUIREMENTS
YOU MUST FOLLOW BEFORE YOU MAY FILE A LAWSUIT FOR
DEFECTIVE CONSTRUCTION AGAINST THE SELLER OR BUILDER
OF YOUR HOME. FORTY-FIVE DAYS BEFORE YOU FILE YOUR
LAWSUIT, YOU MUST DELIVER TO THE SELLER OR BUILDER A
WRITTEN NOTICE OF ANY CONSTRUCTION CONDITIONS YOU
ALLEGE ARE DEFECTIVE AND PROVIDE YOUR SELLER OR BUILDER
THE OPPORTUNITY TO MAKE AN OFFER TO REPAIR OR PAY FOR
THE DEFECTS. YOU ARE NOT OBLIGATED TO ACCEPT ANY OFFER
MADE BY THE BUILDER OR SELLER. THERE ARE STRICT DEADLINES
AND PROCEDURES UNDER STATE LAW, AND FAILURE TO
FOLLOW THEM MAY AFFECT YOUR ABILITY TO FILE A LAWSUIT.

West Virginia
§ 21-11A-5 (a)
requires notice be
given to the owner
of real property upon
entering into a con-
tract for residential
improvements.
§ 21-11A-5(b) requires
that notice be given
in substantially the
format that appears in
the adjoining column.

WEST VIRGINIA STATE LAW, AS SET FORTH IN CHAPTER 21,
ARTICLE 11A OF THE WEST VIRGINIA CODE, CONTAINS
IMPORTANT REQUIREMENTS YOU MUST FOLLOW BEFORE YOU
MAY FILE A LAWSUIT FOR DEFECTIVE CONSTRUCTION AGAINST
THE CONTRACTOR WHO MADE RESIDENTIAL IMPROVEMENTS
TO YOUR PROPERTY. AT LEAST NINETY DAYS BEFORE YOU FILE
YOUR LAWSUIT, YOU MUST DELIVER TO THE CONTRACTOR A
WRITTEN NOTICE OF ANY CONSTRUCTION CONDITIONS YOU
ALLEGE ARE DEFECTIVE AND PROVIDE YOUR CONTRACTOR AND
ANY SUBCONTRACTORS, SUPPLIERS OR DESIGN PROFESSIONALS
THE OPPORTUNITY TO MAKE AN OFFER TO REPAIR OR PAY
FOR THE DEFECTS. YOU ARE NOT OBLIGATED TO ACCEPT ANY
OFFER MADE BY THE CONTRACTOR OR ANY SUBCONTRACTORS,
SUPPLIERS OR DESIGN PROFESSIONALS. THERE ARE DEADLINES
AND PROCEDURES UNDER STATE LAW AND FAILURE TO
FOLLOW THEM MAY AFFECT YOUR ABILITY TO FILE A LAWSUIT.

the section discussing alternative dispute settlement procedures. Specify in the contract with the customer that the customer must provide written notice of any pending warranty claim or defect claim and must offer you an opportunity to inspect and/or make repairs. Such NOR provisions could be a first step on a dispute-resolution continuum before you proceed to alternative dispute-resolution procedures, such as mediation or arbitration.

Figure 6.3 provides an example of a contract provision for NOR that you may adapt to meet your needs and include in your contract. This example is not to replace or alter NOR language in states with NOR statutes. Be sure to check your state for all mandatory requirements.

FIGURE 6.3

Sample Contract Provision for Notice and Opportunity to Repair

The parties agree to be bound by the following procedure in the resolution of any construction defect claim for which the owner contends the builder or remodeler should be liable or responsible under any express warranty provision, statutory warranty requirement, or implied warranty (including an implied warranty of habitability or an implied warranty of workmanlike construction); under any allegation of negligence, misrepresentation, or fraud; or under any other asserted grounds.

1. The home owner shall serve the builder or remodeler with a written notice of any asserted construction defect and shall specify the nature of the asserted defect. Any additions or modifications to the description of the asserted defect(s) shall require the service of an additional written notice, as provided herein.
2. Upon service of the written notice, the owner shall provide the builder or remodeler with reasonable and timely access to the premises for inspection of the asserted defect(s). The builder or remodeler shall undertake the Inspection not more than ____ days from the date of service. The builder or remodeler shall respond to the owner in writing not more than ____ days from the date of inspection. The builder's or remodeler's written response shall include an offer to remedy or repair the asserted defect and/or an offer to settle the claim by monetary payment or provide a denial of liability or responsibility for the asserted claim. The failure of the builder or remodeler to inspect and/or respond as provided herein or the denial by the builder or remodeler of liability or responsibility shall permit the owner to take immediate action to arbitrate any asserted construction defect claim set forth in the written notice. In the absence of other alternative dispute resolution procedures in the contract, the owner may litigate the previously mentioned claim.
3. The owner agrees to accept any reasonable offer made by the builder or remodeler to remedy, repair, and/or to pay such *monetary damages* as may be proximately caused by the construction defect. If any *consequential damages* are excluded under the provisions of an express limited warranty provided under this contract, the monetary damages,

(continued)

FIGURE **6.3**

Sample Contract Provision for Notice and Opportunity to Repair (*Continued*)

described above, shall not include payment of those excluded consequential damages. The failure of the owner to accept a reasonable offer made by the builder or remodeler shall limit any recovery by the owner to the express terms of the builder's or remodeler's reasonable offer. Upon acceptance by the owner, the builder or remodeler shall have ____ days to comply with the terms of the accepted offer.

4. The owner agrees to take no action to initiate arbitration and/or agrees not to file suit in any court of law against the builder or remodeler pertaining to any construction defect claim unless and until the above-stated procedures have been followed and the prescribed time periods have expired without resolution as provided herein. Failure to adhere to these procedures and the prescribed periods shall serve as grounds for summary dismissal, without prejudice, of any arbitration proceeding or lawsuit filed by the owner against the builder or remodeler pertaining to any construction defect claim.

5. Any applicable statute of limitations shall be tolled for the time necessary to comply with the procedures and prescribed time periods set forth above. The remainder of the period of the applicable statute of limitations, if any, shall resume its run upon completion of the repairs in question. The parties specifically agree that these repairs shall not serve to start an entirely new statute of limitations or warranty period. Only the remainder of the original statute of limitations or warranty period will be in effect upon completion of repairs. The parties specifically agree that any and all efforts by the builder or remodeler to remedy or repair any asserted construction defect shall not operate to extend (except as provided herein) any applicable statute of limitations, shall not cause a new statute of limitations period to commence from the date of any repair, and shall not cause a new statute of limitations to commence or be created on account of any remedy or repair effort. The parties specifically agree that any and all efforts by the builder or remodeler to remedy or repair any asserted construction defect shall not extend (except as provided herein) any existing warranty period and shall not create a new period of warranty.

6. Any written notice or response required here shall be served by first class mail, postage prepaid, at the following respective addresses:

Builder or Remodeler: Owner:

_____   _____

_____   _____
(Street)   (Street)

_____   _____
(City, state, and zip)   (City, state, and zip)

7

ALTERNATIVE DISPUTE RESOLUTION

W hen a dispute arises between a builder or remodeler and customer, either during or after construction, they have several dispute resolution methods. Traditionally, parties to a dispute attempt to negotiate a settlement between them (usually with the assistance of their respective lawyers), or they file a lawsuit to have a court resolve the case. As litigation became more expensive and courts became backlogged with cases, alternative means to resolve disputes emerged. Alternative dispute resolution (ADR) provides the parties involved in a dispute with ways to resolve it other than traditional litigation in a court. ADR has an added advantage in that disputes are generally resolved more quickly and cost effectively than litigation procedures.

If you include a form of ADR in your warranty documents or contracts, explain to your customers using alternative dispute resolution methods might be more effective than litigation. Outside of a traditional lawsuit, two of the most recognized methods for resolving legal disputes involve mediation and arbitration.

Mediation

This form of ADR provides a procedure in which a mediator, agreed to by the parties, assists them in reaching an agreement or settlement without deciding who is right or wrong. A mediator is usually a neutral third party who meets with both parties separately and then together and works with them to negotiate a settlement. Mediation is strictly voluntary, and if one of the parties decides not to participate, the other cannot compel participation. The three advantages are it is less expensive, the proceedings remain confidential, and it can reduce barriers to communication between the involved parties. Mediation is especially desirable as a dispute-resolution option when the parties want to maintain an ongoing relationship.

Arbitration

By contrast, in arbitration, the parties submit their case to a neutral third person or a panel of individuals (arbitrators) for a final resolution. As with mediation, arbitration provides a mechanism for resolving disputes without the expense and delay that generally occur in a lawsuit. Arbitration is a recognized method of dispute resolution in all 50 states. Typically, arbitration is final and binding, and neither party can appeal the decision except in the case of impropriety or fraud by the arbitrator. The binding nature of arbitration can be a disadvantage in that it does not allow an appeal of the arbitrator's findings.

Conversely, the case has an end date without the expense of seemingly endless appeals by the unsuccessful party. The tailored needs of the contracting parties make arbitration a popular option. Usually, parties will jointly select an arbitrator and the manner in which the arbitration will proceed. In addition, the parties can choose arbitrators who specialize in a particular type of case, such as construction or labor.

Because arbitration requires parties to waive their constitutional right to a jury trial, courts will strictly construe mandatory arbitration clauses in all contracts. If courts find an arbitration clause vague or ambiguous, it is likely to be unenforceable. Some states require arbitration clauses are printed in a typeface that is bigger than the typeface in the rest of the contract. Others may require that the clause is in a conspicuous place or that the contracting parties separately initial or sign it.

If courts find an arbitration clause vague or ambiguous, they generally will not enforce it.

If a contract includes an arbitration clause and if the subject of the contract involves interstate commerce, like using building materials shipped across state lines, the Federal Arbitration Act (FAA) governs the arbitration clause. In the event of a conflict between the FAA and state law, the FAA preempts (trumps) state law. Both the FAA and all individual state arbitration acts provide that if a contract has a valid arbitration clause, one party may compel the other into an arbitration proceeding.

Controversy surrounds the use of arbitration clauses in contracts because some people believe that these clauses are unconscionable, oppressive to homeowners, or unreasonably favorable to the builder or remodeler. To help minimize the chances that a customer challenges your clause as unconscionable, or otherwise invalid, consider the following:

- Make the arbitration clause in your contract obvious—have the customers initial the clause indicating that they have read and understood it.
- Do not limit remedies in the arbitration clause. Ensure your clause does not deprive the customers of any remedies they would otherwise have in a court of law. If you want to use binding arbitration, inform the customers so that they know they cannot appeal the arbitrator's decision.
- Have your attorney review your arbitration clause to ensure that it contains the appropriate language, proper typeface and/or font size, correct location within the contract, and endorsement requirements for your jurisdiction.
- Be sure the clause does not favor you at the expense of your customers.
- If a customer cannot pay the filing fees, consider paying the fees or a portion of them.
- The arbitration hearing should take place near where the property/house is situated.
- The arbitrator should be neutral without ties to the builder, the building industry, or to the customer. Usually both parties participate in the selection, so involve the customer in selecting the arbitrator.

ADR has grown significantly in popularity over the years. Many state courts have procedures to require some form of ADR, such as mediation, before a case can proceed. In addition, it is a requirement for all U.S. District Courts to provide ADR procedures for litigants. These procedures may include mediation, settlement conferences, early neutral evaluation, nonbinding summary jury trial, corporate minitrial, and arbitration proceedings. If both parties consent, the Alternative Dispute Resolution Act of 1998 (28 U.S.C. §§ 651 *et seq.*) authorizes federal district courts to refer cases to arbitration.

Many organizations also offer ADR services. The American Arbitration Association is one of the most recognized organizations. This nonprofit organization provides mediation and arbitration services for parties involved in disputes. The AAA has rules and procedures for large and small construction related claims and disputes, including fast-track procedures for claims involving no more than $75,000. The fast-track procedures include a standard of 60 days to complete cases, using prequalified arbitrators to hear cases on an expedited basis, appointing an arbitrator more quickly, limiting the number of hearing days (usually to 1 day), and announcing an award no more than 14 calendar days after the conclusion of the hearing.

If you decide to include an arbitration clause in your contract, consider these two additional points when drafting that clause: (a) decide what rules you want to use in the event arbitration is necessary and (b) determine whether your state requires procedures for arbitration. For example, you could:

- Select procedures and rules established by the AAA regarding construction-related claims.
- Choose local arbitration rules or guidelines offered by the courts in the jurisdiction of the dispute.
- Select procedures established by local organizations that offer ADR services.
- Adopt procedures on an ad hoc basis by drafting a set to include directly in your contract.
- Allow the arbitrators to adopt their own procedures to handle your dispute.

The downside to the last two options is that such ad hoc procedures burden the parties to agree on how to proceed and administer the arbitration once a dispute arises. The procedures could ultimately prove unsatisfactory.

As mentioned above, you should state that the location of the arbitration hearing would be near the property or site. Consider including a choice-of-law provision if (a) your business is operating outside of its home state, (b) the other party is from a different state, or (c) the property is located on or near a border. A choice-of-law provision allows application of the chosen state's law and procedures to govern the conduct of the arbitration.

You may want to incorporate the following additional considerations in an arbitration clause:

- Allow some limited discovery and production of documents during the course of the arbitration. These procedures may help to strengthen your case and clarify the issues and claims for the arbitrators.
- Provide interim relief pending the arbitrator's final decision to help assuage objections to the arbitration process.
- Consolidate the case if the claim involves more than two parties. Consolidation could be an option for you in the event that multiple parties become involved in a dispute, such as if the owner tries to sue you, the materials suppliers, and trade contractors.
- Set reasonable time limitations for the process to begin to avoid lengthy delays in commencing and concluding the process.

- Designate who will be responsible for costs and expenses related to the arbitration, including attorneys' fees and the apportion of costs, to alleviate any potential unknowns from the arbitration process.

Ultimately, setting out procedures in advance gives both parties an opportunity to review the procedures you want to use in your business and provides the customer a realistic expectation regarding the overall dispute resolution process.

8

STATUTORY WARRANTIES

In addition to implied warranties, some states have enacted statutory new home warranties. Statutory warranties are imposed on new home construction and sales by an act of the state legislature. They add another regulation that builders must comply with when conducting business in states with these statutes. Only fourteen states currently have some form of statutory warranties for new single family home construction.*

Statutory warranty provisions usually impose differing limitation periods for warranty coverage on listed components of a new home.

Although little uniformity exists among these states' statutory warranties, these acts provide standards of construction like a term of warranty duration, a claims procedure for home purchasers, and legal remedies intended to resolve construction defect issues involving their new homes.

California, Cal. Civil Code § 895–§ 945.5

California's warranty statutes (also known as S.B. 800) are more extensive than Connecticut's. California sets building standards for defects with respect to water issues. The standards list the specific building components and their systems that water shall not pass beyond, around, or through, nor collect through excessive condensation. California's statutes also set standards for other aspects of construction that include:

- Structural components.
- Plumbing and sewer.
- Soil issues.

- Electrical systems.
- Fire protection.

---

* As of press date.

With few exceptions, most components (labor and materials) have a 10-year warranty. Exceptions include the following:

Five-Year Statutory Warranty

- Paint applications

Four-Year Statutory Warranty

- Electrical system
- Driveways
- Plumbing and sewer systems
- Sidewalks and patios
- Untreated steel fences

Two-Year Statutory Warranty

- Untreated wood posts
- Dryer ducts

One-Year Statutory Warranty

- Drainage systems
- Inter-unit noise transmission
- Fit and finish issues
  - Cabinets
  - Countertops
  - Mirrors
  - Paint finishes
  - Flooring
  - Trim
  - Interior and exterior walls

The California statutes include extensive provisions for claims and remedies. California's notice and opportunity to repair laws are in these same statutes.

Connecticut, Conn. Gen. Stat. Ann. § 47-116–§ 47-121

The Connecticut New Home Warranties Act codifies the following implied warranties that apply in every home sale, so that the home is:

- Free from faulty materials.
- Constructed according to sound engineering principles.
- Constructed in a workmanlike manner.
- Fit for habitation when the deed is delivered.

These warranties terminate one year after delivery or taking possession, whichever occurs first.

An additional statutory implied warranty in Connecticut requires that the builder comply with all building code provisions. Claimants have three years from the date of the certificate of occupancy to bring an action under this statutory warranty.

Georgia, Ga. Code § 43-41-7

Georgia requires licensed residential contractors to offer a written warranty in connection with each contract to construct, superintend or manage the construction of any single-family residence when the total value of the work, activity, or compensation exceeds $2,500.00. In addition, Georgia's Administrative Code provides more detail on what the written warranty must contain, including that it describe covered work and activities, exclusions, standards for evaluating work and activities (which standards shall be those set forth in the current edition of the Residential Construction Performance Guidelines as published by NAHB, the term of the warranty including commencement dates or events, procedures for making a claim, the contractor's response options (repair, replace or compensate), assignable manufacturer warranties, as well as attaching a complete copy of the written warranty to the contract, or make that warranty available for review. *See,* Ga. Comp. R. & Regs. 553-7-.01.

Hawaii

Hawaii does not require that warranties be provided on home construction or home improvements. However, if a contractor does provide a warranty, the Hawaii Administrative Rules require the contractor to disclose all warranties to the homeowner prior to obtaining a binding contract from the homeowner and prior to applying for a building permit. *See* Haw. Admin. Rules § 16-77-79(a)(4).

Indiana, Ind. Code § 32-27-2-1–§ 32-27-2-11

Indiana provides statutory warranties for improvements to existing homes and for new home construction. The statutory warranty provisions establish three different warranty periods depending on the defect or component.

A two-year warranty period provides that the home is free from defects caused by (a) faulty workmanship or defective materials and (b) faulty installation of plumbing, electrical, heating, cooling, or ventilating systems (excluding fixtures, appliances, or equipment items). A four-year warranty period covers faulty workmanship or defective materials in the roof or roofing systems, and a 10-year warranty period covers major structural defects. Indiana also extends its statutory warranty coverage to subsequent purchasers.

Effective July 1, 2023, amendments to the Indiana code now include statutory warranties for builders selling model homes. Builders may warrant the model home for a 10-year period, and the warranty applies to subsequent home buyers. The statute requires the home buyer who purchased the model home to notify the subsequent purchaser of the warranty date and the amount of time remaining on the warranty. *See,* Ind. Code § 32-27-2-8.5.

Indiana does not require builders extend these statutory warranties to their customers. However, by law, only those builders who expressly provide these statutory warranties are permitted to disclaim the common law implied warranty of fitness for habitability. This common law implied-warranty runs for a period of 10 years from the point of substantial completion for all defects in materials or labor that fall within the purview of the implied warranty.

Louisiana, La. Rev. Stat. Ann. § 9:3141–§ 9:3150

In Louisiana, the New Home Warranty Act provides coverage "whether or not building code regulations are in effect in the location of the structure." Louisiana's warranty act applies to "any defect," even though no building standard may directly regulate the defective workmanship or materials. Statutory provisions (similar to Indiana's) provide different warranty durations for different parts of a new home. The statutory one-year warranty period covers noncompliance with building standards or other defects in materials or workmanship. The two-year statutory warranty period covers plumbing, electrical, heating, cooling, and ventilating systems but excludes appliances, fixtures, and equipment. The five-year statutory warranty period covers major structural defects resulting from either noncompliance with building standards or other defects in materials or workmanship.

"Warranty commencement date" means the date that legal title to a home is conveyed to its initial purchaser or the date the home is first occupied, whichever occurs first.

Unless the parties otherwise agree in writing, the builder's warranty shall exclude the following items:

(1) Fences, landscaping, including but not limited to sodding, seeding, shrubs, existing and new trees, plantings, off-site improvements, all

driveways and walkways, or any other improvement not a part of the home itself.

(2) After the first year, the concrete floor of a basement and the concrete floor of an attached or unattached garage that is built separate from a foundation wall or other structural element of the home.

(3) Damage to real property that is not part of the home or purchase price of the home covered by the warranty.

Applies to subsequent purchasers, but this does not extend the duration of any warranty or insurance coverage.

Maine, Me. Rev. Stat. Ann. §1487(10.)

The Maine Home Construction Contracts Act requires all contracts for building a residence more than $3,000 be in writing and signed by the builder and the purchaser. Every such contract must contain a warranty statement which reads:

> In addition to any additional warranties agreed to by the parties, the contractor warrants that the work will be free from faulty materials; constructed according to the standards of the building code applicable for this location; constructed in a skillful manner and fit for habitation or appropriate use. The warranty rights and remedies set forth in the Maine Uniform Commercial Code apply to this contract.

The parties to a home construction contract can exclude the statutory warranty provision if the contractor specifically "informs the purchaser of his rights under the Act, and the parties then agree to a contract that does not contain the statutory warranty provision."

Maryland, Md. Code Ann., Real Prop. § 10-604–§ 10-610

Maryland's New Home Warranties Act requires every builder to disclose in writing prior to entering into a contract for the construction of a new home whether or not the builder participates in "a new home security plan." Participants must provide owners with a new home warranty in accordance with the provisions of the statute. Builders who do not participate in a new home security plan must include a statutory disclosure of this fact in their contracts and provide the prospective purchaser with a five-day right of rescission from the contract date. Participant builders must provide a "Notice to Purchaser" concerning the warranty in their new home contracts. See text in Figure 6.2 States That Require Mandatory Notices.

At a minimum, each new home warranty extended by builders who participate in a security plan must provide the following:

- For one year, the new home is free from any defects in materials and workmanship.
- For two years, the new home is free from any defect in the electrical, plumbing, heating, cooling, and ventilating systems. However, for appliances, the warranty may not exceed the length and scope of the manufacturer's warranty.
- For five years, the new home is free from any structural defect.

The statutory warranty may exclude certain claims, including bodily injury or damage to personal items, any damage the owner has not taken timely efforts to minimize, normal deterioration, and damage caused by third-party grading.

By statute, in every contract for the initial sale of a new home, a Maryland builder must include a provision that the new home will be constructed in accordance with performance standards or guidelines that are, at a minimum, the performance standards or guidelines that have been adopted by the National Association of Home Builders. In Maryland, NAHB's *Residential Construction Performance Guidelines* provide the performance standards of construction, and define what constitutes a "defect" for statutory warranty purposes. *See* MD Code, Real Property, § 14-117(j)(3)1.

Minnesota, Minn. Stat. § 327A.01–§ 327A.08

Minnesota's statutory warranties extend to home improvements and new homes. The statutory warranties also apply to subsequent purchasers. Minnesota sets a one-year warranty period for home improvements covering defects caused by "faulty workmanship and defective materials resulting from noncompliance with building standards." For an improvement involving "plumbing, electrical, heating, or cooling systems," the warranty period is two years for defects caused by "faulty installation" resulting from "noncompliance with building standards." The warranty duration is ten years for "major construction defects due to noncompliance with building standards. Minnesota excludes certain claims from warranty coverage, including:

- Secondary personal injury or property damage.
- Loss or damage from dampness and condensation resulting from insufficient ventilation after occupancy.
- Landscaping or insect damage.

▨ Loss or damage caused by defects in design, installation, or materials supplied or installed by the buyer or owner.

Mississippi, Miss. Code § 83-58-1–§ 83-58-17

The Mississippi statutes provide that every builder warrants the following to a new homeowner:

▨ For one-year, the home will be free "from defects due to noncompliance with building standards."
▨ For six years, the home will be free "from major structural defects due to noncompliance with the building standards."

The Mississippi statutes define the warranty commencement date as the date that legal title is conveyed or when the home is first occupied, whichever occurs first.

The statutory warranties automatically transfer without charge to subsequent purchasers.

Mississippi statutory warranty exclusions include defects in detached outbuildings, swimming pools, driveways, patios, retaining walls, landscaping, and any improvement not part of the home. The statute also excludes mold damage, except when the builder's negligence was a proximate cause of the mold or the mold damage.

New Jersey, N.J. Stat. Ann. § 46:3B-1–46:3B-20

The New Jersey New Home Warranty and Builders' Registration Act provides a one-year warranty that the residence "shall be free from defects caused by faulty workmanship and defective materials due to noncompliance with the building standards." A two-year warranty covers a faulty install of plumbing, electrical, heating, and cooling systems. (Appliance coverage does not extend beyond the length and scope of the manufacturers' warranties.) A 10-year statutory warranty period protects homeowners against major construction defects. The Act defines "major construction defects" as "any actual damage to the load-bearing portion of the home, including damage due to subsidence, expansion or lateral movement of the soil which affects its load bearing function." This definition excludes soil movement caused by flood or earthquake.

The New Jersey Act also establishes a new home warranty security fund that provides money sufficient to pay owners' claims against builders who participate in the fund, for defects in homes covered by the statutory new home warranty. Before making a claim for these funds, it requires an owner to notify the builder and allow a reasonable time period for repair.

New York, N.Y. Gen. Bus. § 777–§ 777(b)

New York statutorily creates "a housing merchant implied warranty that is implied in the contract for the sale of every new home." The housing merchant implied warranty also transfers to subsequent purchasers. The housing merchant implied-warranty means the following:

- For one year after the warranty date, the home will be "free from defects due to a failure to construct it in a skillful manner."
- For two years after the warranty date, the plumbing, electrical, heating, cooling, and ventilation systems will be "free from defects due to failure to install in a skillful manner."
- For six years from the warranty date, the home will be free from material defects (actual physical damage to specified load-bearing portions of the home).

In the case of appliances included in the sale of the new home, the housing merchant implied warranty applies only to defects caused by a failure to install in a skillful manner and not to issues of merchantability or fitness. The uniform commercial code governs issues involving warrantability or fitness.

The warranty date is measured from the passing of title or occupancy, whichever occurs first. The housing merchant implied warranty may be excluded or modified by the builder or seller, but only if the builder or seller offers the buyer a limited warranty that meets or exceeds specific standards and provisions that are set out in the Act.

Nevada, N.R.S. 624.602

Nevada warranty requirements for new homes are:

(a) Nevada requires that the warranty be in writing.
(b) The warranty must be valid for a period of at least 1 year from the date of completion of a written punch list. "Punch list" means a list of any materials or work describing incomplete or incorrect installations or incidental damage to existing finishes, material and structures that do not conform to the specifications of the contract or the requirements of subsection 1 of NRS 624.3017.
(c) The warranty must contain terms that include, without limitation, warrantying all home systems, workmanship, materials, plumbing, electrical

and mechanical systems, appliances installed by contractors, fixtures, equipment, and structural components, unless a separate warranty is provided by the manufacturer or installer of such a product, component or system.

(d) The warranty must be transferable to a subsequent purchaser of the residence.

(e) Lastly, the warranty is not to be deemed, construed, or interpreted to constitute a waiver or release of any other warranty from the licensee provided by contract or otherwise available under the laws of Nevada.

Texas

Formally, Texas had a statutory warranty requirement overseen by the Texas Residential Construction Commission. In 2009, the Commission was subject to sunset review, and the Texas legislation did not pass legislation that would have allowed the Commission to continue existing. Now, Texas does not have any statutory warranty requirements.

Virginia, Va. Code Ann. § 55.1-357

This Virginia Code provision imposes an implied warranty in the contract for the sale of every new dwelling. The vendor impliedly warrants that the dwelling and all its fixtures are free from structural defects and are constructed in a workmanlike manner to pass without objection in the trade. If the vendor is in the business of building or selling homes, the law also imposes an implied warranty that the dwelling is fit for habitation. These implied warranties extend to subsequent purchasers.

All of Virginia's statutory implied warranties last for a period of one year from the date of title transfer or the taking of possession, whichever occurs first, except for defects involving the new dwelling's foundation, for which the implied warranty lasts for five years.

These Virginia statutory implied warranties may be waived or modified, but only if the disclaimer is set forth conspicuously on the face of the contract in capital letters that are at least two points larger than the other type in the contract. In addition, the language must specifically state which implied warranties are being waived or excluded. This provision has been strictly construed by Virginia courts.

A disclaimer of implied warranties that was conspicuous and in capital letters was nonetheless ruled as ineffective because the type size was *not* two points larger.

A list of the states with statutory warranties and their respective code sections appear in Figure 8.1.

FIGURE 8.1

States with Statutory New Home Warranties*

State	Code Sections
California	Civil Code § 895–§ 945.5
Connecticut	§ 47-116–§ 47-121
Georgia	§ 43-41-7
Hawaii	Haw. Admin. Rules § 16-77-79(a)(4)++
Indiana[†]	§ 32-27-2-1–§ 32-27-2-11
Louisiana	§ 9:3141–§ 9:3150
Maine[†]	§ 1487(10.)
Maryland[†]	Real Property Code § 10-604–§ 10-610 (except Montgomery County)
Minnesota	§ 327A.01–§ 327A.08
Mississippi	§ 83-58-1–§ 83-58-17
New Jersey	§ 46:3B-1–46:3B-20
New York	General Business Law § 777–§ 777(b)
Nevada	Nevada Rev. Stat. § 624.602
Virginia[†]	§ 55.1-357*

* As of press date.

† Allows waiver or nonuse of statutory warranty. May require a contract disclaimer containing specific language and/or format and acknowledgment of the purchaser.

++ If a contractor provides a warranty then he or she must disclose all warranties to the homeowner prior to signing the contract.

CHAPTER 9

WARRANTIES MANDATED BY HUD

Approximately one-third of the new homes constructed each year have a third-party insurance-backed 10-year home warranty covering the structural integrity of the home. The U.S. Department of Housing and Urban Development (HUD) previously required borrowers to receive a 10-year home warranty plan to qualify for FHA mortgage insurance on certain high loan-to-value mortgages and reviewed and approved 10-year home warranty plans.

On December 14, 2018, HUD published a final rule entitled the "Streamlining Warranty Requirements for Federal Housing Administration (FHA) Single-Family Mortgage Insurance: Removal of the Ten-Year Protection Plan Requirements." With this rule, effective March 14, 2019, HUD eliminated the requirement for borrowers to receive a 10-year protection plan to qualify for FHA mortgage insurance and ceased setting standards for and approving home warranty plans. While home warranty companies are subject to individual state requirements and regulation, and the Departments of Veterans Affairs and Agriculture still have home warranty requirements, there are no longer nationally recognized guidelines from HUD.

10

THE MAGNUSON-MOSS WARRANTY ACT

In 1975, Congress enacted the Magnuson-Moss Warranty Act in response to extensive abuses by merchants concerning express and implied warranties and disclaimers. Congress designed the Act to prevent abuse of written warranties and service contracts for consumer products. The Act defines consumer products as including "any tangible personal property . . . which is normally used for personal, family, or household purposes (including any such property intended to be attached to or installed in any real property without regard to whether it is so attached or installed)." 15 U.S.C. § 2301(1).

Congress named the Federal Trade Commission (FTC) the agency charged with regulating warranties on consumer products under the Magnuson-Moss Warranty Act. The Act does not require builders or remodelers to provide their customers with a warranty. It regulates the form of whatever warranty a builder or remodeler may *voluntarily* choose to provide. The Act applies to builder-backed warranties and insured warranty programs, such as manufacturers' warranties. It states that, to be valid, these warranties must meet certain disclosure requirements. These requirements do not apply to new or remodeled houses. Instead, they apply only to the following consumer items installed or included in new or remodeled houses: appliances, manufactured equipment, air conditioners, furnaces, water heaters, and anything else defined as *consumer products* under the Act.

Building materials sold over the counter at a home improvement or building supply store could be considered products. However, if a builder or remodeler incorporates the building materials into a home or building, the Act does not consider them consumer products because they cannot be practically distinguished from the realty. 16 C.F.R. § 700.1(e).

When a builder or remodeler makes improvements to an existing structure, the nature of the materials used may determine whether they are part of the real estate or deemed a consumer product for purposes of the Act. The regulations provide that "the intention of the parties [is] to contract for the construction of realty which will integrate the component materials." 16 C.F.R. § 700.1(f). New windows, doors, or a patio may be considered consumer products if they are attached separately as items of equipment.

One of the earliest cases applying the Magnuson-Moss Act in a construction context is *Muchisky v. Frederic Roofing Co., Inc.,* 838 S.W.2d 74 (Mo. Ct. App. 1992). In *Muchisky,* the written contract to reroof the home contained a 12-year, defect-free warranty that the completed roof "would be free from defects in workmanship and materials." *Id.* at 75. The court ruled that the Act covers the warranty provided on the installation of a replacement roof. The issue before the court involved whether the reroofing of a home was a consumer product as defined by the Act. The court ruled that because the roofing materials were an improvement to the *existing structure,* the new roofing materials were consumer products. *Id.* at 77–79. The court distinguished between products *added* to an existing structure from those products used to *create* a structure. *Id.* at 78. In this case, the court held that the breach of the warranty entitled the homeowner to damages and attorney's fees. *Id.* at 78.

Thus, items of equipment added to a new house or a major addition (such as the improvement in *Muchisky*) that possess a function *separate* from the realty are subject to the Act. When builders and remodelers integrate building materials, such as windows, doors, dropped ceilings, and siding, into the structure of a dwelling, these products are not consumer products and are not subject to the Act. The nature of the transaction offers guidance on whether the Act applies. Building materials purchased over the counter from a building supply store are consumer products covered by the Act. If these materials become indistinguishable from the real property, the Act does not apply. Going back to the *Muchisky* case, if the contractor used the roofing materials as part of a substantial remodeling project or major addition, or for a new house, the materials would not be subject to the Act. *See McFadden v. Dryvit Systems, Inc.,* 2004 WL 2278542 (D. Or. October 8, 2004) (Holding that an EIFS system that was purchased and installed on an already existing home was a "consumer product" for the purposes of the Magnuson-Moss

Items of equipment added to a new house or a major addition that possess a function separate from the realty are subject to the Act.

Warranty Act). See also. *Atkinson v. Elk Corporation of Texas*, 48 Cal. Rptr. 3d 247 (2006) (Citing *Muchisky* with approval and finding that "With respect to products that are incorporated into realty, we find that the crucial distinction is the *time of sale*. If the products are purchased in order to add them to an existing dwelling, then the products are consumer products. If, on the other hand, the products are purchased as part of a larger real estate sales contract, or contract for a *substantial* addition to a home, they are not); *Miller v. Herman*, 600 F.3d 726 (7th Cir. 2010) (Under the facts of this case, "windows" were not a "consumer product" under the Magnuson-Moss Act - Miller contracted with Herman for the construction of a new home. The home was not existing; the windows at issue here were purchased by Herman, a contractor, to install into the home. Miller has not produced any evidence showing a separate contract for the windows, or a separate transaction for them in which he was personally engaged); *Haley v. Kolbe & Kolbe Millwork Co., Inc.* 2015 WL 9255571 (W.D. Wis. 2015) (Windows ordered by a builder as part of the construction of a new home are not considered consumer products).

Warranty provisions that cover consumer products must comply with the Federal Trade Commission regulations. When deciding whether to provide a warranty, consider your responsibilities under the Magnuson-Moss Act. In making this decision, you have three options:

- Give no written warranty at all, which may not be practical in many markets.
- Exclude consumer products entirely from any warranty you do provide. By excluding consumer products, you will avoid triggering the Magnuson-Moss requirements. However, keep in mind that by excluding these products, you will necessarily exclude an enormous variety of appliances and pieces of equipment.
- If you do provide warranties, be sure that they conform to the Magnuson-Moss requirements.

Because the Act applies only if a warranty covers consumer products, a warranty that excludes *all* consumer products from coverage is not affected by the Act. You might use the following examples of language to exclude consumer products from your written warranty:

Example 1

"This warranty does not cover any appliance, piece of equipment, or other item . . . [that] is a consumer product for purposes of the Magnuson-Moss Warranty Act." (15 U.S.C. §§ 2301–2312).

Example 2

"This warranty does not cover any appliance, piece of equipment, or other item in the home, that is a 'consumer product' for the purposes of the Magnuson-Moss Warranty Act (15 U.S.C. §§ 2301–2312). The following are examples of 'consumer products,' but . . . other items in the home . . . also [may be] consumer products:" (List the items from the FTC list (Figure 10.1).)

Of these two examples, Example 2 offers more legal protection, but including it in a short warranty document may be awkward.

Excluding appliances and pieces of equipment from a written warranty will prevent those items from being subject to the FTC's requirements regarding form and language. However, if the warranty exclusions limit the warranty's scope and application too much or if they leave nothing covered, the FTC could consider the warranty a sham under Section 5 of the Federal Trade Commission Act, which covers "unfair and deceptive acts and practices."

Because the Act pertains primarily to the form of a warranty rather than to your obligations, the easiest solution might be to write your warranty

FIGURE **10.1**
___

Federal Trade Commission Regulation Requirements for Warranty Documents

For these requirements, see the Code of Federal Regulations (C.F.R.) Title 16, Part 701 or 16 C.F.R. § 701.3—Written warranty terms:

- The name and address of the party giving the warranty (warrantor).
- The name of the person who is receiving the warranty and whether it is transferable to subsequent purchasers.
- Precisely what the warranty covers and what it does not cover.
- What the warrantor will do if a warranted defect or problem occurs and how much the consumer will have to pay.
- The duration of the warranty and when it begins.
- Information regarding availability of any informal dispute settlement procedures elected by the warrantor.
- Limitations on consequential or secondary results must stand out clearly and conspicuously from the rest of the document, and these exact words must follow the limitations: "Some states do not allow the exclusion or limitation of incidental or consequential damages, so the above limitation or exclusion may not apply to you."
- Limitations on the duration of implied warranty rights also must appear in clear and unmistakable language, and they must be prominently displayed on the face of the warranty document, along with the statement: "Some states do not allow limitations on how long an implied warranty lasts, so this limitation may not apply to you."
- A provision stating: "This warranty gives you specific legal rights, and you may also have other rights, which may vary from state to state."

using the form required by the Act. Although this form may go beyond what the law requires, using the act's format ensures that your warranty document complies with the Act.

If the Magnuson-Moss Act covers any part of your warranty and you provide for alternative dispute resolution methods to resolve claims, the warranty must follow the settlement procedures outlined in the Act. The Act authorizes the FTC to regulate devices under which warranty disputes between the warrantor and a consumer are submitted to a third party for mediation or arbitration. The Act refers to these devices as "informal dispute settlement mechanisms."

Although you are not required to provide such a mechanism, if you choose to do so in your warranty document, the mechanism must meet FTC standards. If you provide informal dispute settlement procedures, you receive an added benefit. The Act provides that, (a) if you set up your procedures so that the procedures and implementation meet the requirements of the FTC standards, and (b) you incorporate into your written warranty a requirement that the customer resort to these procedures "before pursuing any legal remedy" regarding the warranty, the customer cannot bring a lawsuit (other than a class action suit) until he or she "initially resorts" to the informal dispute procedures. *See* 15 U.S.C. § 2310(a)(3)(A)–(C). However, if a court determines your procedures are unfair, it may invalidate them. Because these rules are complicated, your attorney should review your warranty documents to ensure they do not conflict with the Act. FTC Dispute Resolution Rules setting out these requirements are at 16 C.F.R. §§ 703.2–703.8 (2005).

If you give a full, written warranty, the Magnuson-Moss Act does not allow you to disclaim implied warranties on consumer products. However, you may limit the implied warranty to the same duration as a written warranty of reasonable duration, as long as the limitation is (a) conscionable, (b) set forth in clear and unmistakable language, and (c) prominently displayed on the front of the warranty.

Unless your state law does not permit this restriction on implied warranties, you can make the duration of the implied warranty the same period as the written warranty. These simple requirements make warranties more understandable to consumers. Some courts are more likely to enforce a limited warranty if it is simple, clear, and easy for a home buyer or homeowner to understand even if the Magnuson-Moss Act does not specifically apply.

Under the FTC regulations, consumers must have access to consumer-product warranties before a sale. Sellers can display the warranty near the warranted product or make it available upon request. Sellers who choose to make warranties available upon request must post signs to that effect, and the warranty document must include the information in the list in Figure 10.1.

Statutes of Repose Applicable to Construction Claims by State

These statutes are current as of press date. Please be advised that statutes can and do change through amendment, repeal, or new legislation. Builders and remodelers should check the current state code for the statutory provisions applicable on a given date.

State	Type of Action	Period of Repose	Commencement	Comment	State Code Section
Alabama	Construction defects	7 years	Substantial completion of construction		Ala. Code § 6-5-221
Alaska	Construction defects	10 years	Later of substantial completion of construction or the last act alleged to have caused the injury		Alaska Stat. § 09.10.055
Arizona	Construction defects – contract, implied warranty	8 years	Substantial completion of construction	Maximum of 9 years (additional year granted if defect is discovered in final year)	Ariz. Rev. Stat. § 12-552(A)
Arkansas	Construction defects – injury to property	5 years	Substantial completion of construction		Ark. Code Ann. § 16-56-112(a)
	Construction defects – personal injury and wrongful death	4 years	Substantial completion of construction	Maximum of 5 years (additional year granted if defect is discovered in final year)	Ark. Code Ann. § 16-56-112(b)
California	Construction defects – patent defects	4 years	Substantial completion of construction	Maximum of 5 years (additional year granted if defect is discovered in final year)	Cal. Code Civ. Proc. § 337.1
	Construction defects – latent defects	10 years	Substantial completion of construction		Cal. Code Civ. Proc. § 317.15
Colorado	Construction defects	6 years	Substantial completion of construction	Maximum of 8 years (additional 2 years granted if defect is discovered in final 2 years)	Colo. Rev. Stat. § 13-80-104(1)
Connecticut	Construction defects – contracts	7 years	Substantial completion		Conn. Gen. Stat. § 52-584a
	Construction defects – torts	3 years	Act or omission complained of		Conn. Gen. Stat. § 52-584
Delaware	Construction defects	6 years	Generally, substantial completion of construction, acceptance of the home, or the date when final payment is received		Del. Code Ann. tit. 10, § 8127
District of Columbia	Construction defects	10 years	Substantial completion of construction	Does not apply to contract actions	D.C. Code Ann. § 12-310

State	Type of Action	Period of Repose	Commencement	Comment	State Code Section
Florida	Construction defects	7 years	The earlier of (i) the date of issuance of a temporary certificate of occupancy (TCO), a certificate of occupancy, or a certificate of completion; or (ii) the date of abandonment if construction is not completed.	There is a different commencement period for model homes and multi-building projects.	Fla. Stat. Ann. § 95.11(3)(c)
Georgia	Construction defects	8 years	Substantial completion of construction	Maximum of 10 years (additional 2 years granted if defect is discovered in final 2 years). Does not apply to actions for breach of express contractual warranties.	Ga. Code Ann. § 9-3-51
Hawaii	Construction defects	10 years	Substantial completion of construction or abandonment		Haw. Rev. Stat. § 657-8
Idaho	Construction defects – torts	6 years	Final completion of construction	*See West v. El Paso Prods. Co.,* 122 Idaho 133 (Idaho 1992) (holding that § 5-241 is a statute of repose).	Idaho Code § 5-241
	Construction defects – written contract	5 years	Final completion of construction	*See West v. El Paso Prods. Co.,* 122 Idaho 133 (Idaho 1992) (holding that § 5-241 is a statute of repose).	Idaho Code § 5-241; § 5-216
Illinois	Construction defects	10 years	Act or omission giving rise to the cause of action	Maximum of 14 years (additional 4 years granted if defect is discovered in final 4 years)	735 Ill. Comp. Stat. 5/13-214
Indiana	Construction defects	10 years or 12 years (see Comment)		Period could be extended to 12 years after completion of plans and specifications to the owner if the action is for a deficiency in the design of the improvement.	Ind. Code § 32-30-1-5

State	Type of Action	Period of Repose	Commencement	Comment	State Code Section
Iowa	Construction defects – tort and implied warranties	10 years	After construction is complete	If the unsafe or defective condition is discovered within 1 year prior to the expiration of the applicable period of repose, the period of repose shall be extended one year.	Iowa Code § 614.1(11)* *Does not apply to express warranty claims
Kansas	Construction defects	10 years	Act giving rise to the cause of action		Kan. Stat. Ann. § 60-513
Kentucky	Construction defects	7 years	Substantial completion of construction	Maximum of 8 years (additional year granted if defect is discovered in final year). This statute remains a part of the Kentucky Code, however, this statute of repose was ruled to be unconstitutional by the Kentucky Supreme Court in *Perkins v. Northeastern Log Homes,* 808 S.W.2d 809 (Ky. 1991).	Ky. Rev. Stat. Ann. § 413.135
Louisiana	Construction defects	5 years	Occupancy by the home owner	Maximum of 6 years (additional year granted if defect is discovered in final year)	La. Rev. Stat. Ann. § 9:2772
Maine	Construction defects	6 years	Conveyance from builder to home owner	*See Dunelawn Owners' Ass'n v. Gendreau,* 2000 ME 94, p. 15 (Me. 2000) which states that a purchaser's suit against a builder for latent defects accrues when the house is conveyed; *see also, Bangor Water Dist. V. Malcom Pirnie Engrs.,* 534 A.2d 1326 (Me. 1988) (holding that discovery rule does not apply to contractors).	Me. Rev. Stat. Ann. tit. 14, § 752.

State	Type of Action	Period of Repose	Commencement	Comment	State Code Section
Maryland	Construction defects	10 years	When improvement becomes available for use		Md. Code Ann., Md. Cts. & Jud. Proc. § 5-108(b)
Massachusetts	Construction defects	6 years	Earlier of opening of improvement for use or substantial completion of construction		Mass. Gen. Laws ch. 260, § 2B
Michigan	Construction defects	6 years	Occupancy, use or acceptance by home owner	Maximum of 10 years (additional 4 years granted if defect is the result of gross negligence)	Mich. Comp. Laws § 600.5839
Minnesota	Construction defects	10 years	Substantial completion of construction	Maximum of 12 years (additional 2 years granted if defect is discovered in final 2 years)	Minn. Stat. § 541.051
Mississippi	Construction defects	6 years	Earlier of written acceptance, actual occupancy, or use by home owner		Miss. Code Ann. § 15-1-41
Missouri	Construction defects	10 years	Completion of construction		Mo. Rev. Stat. § 516.097
Montana	Construction defects	10 years	Completion of construction	Maximum of 11 years (additional year granted if defect is discovered in final year). This statute of repose does not apply to contract actions.	Mont. Code Ann. § 27-2-208
Nebraska	Construction defects	5 years	Act or omission giving rise to cause of action	Does not apply to contract actions	Neb. Rev. Stat. § 25-223(2)(a)
Nevada	Construction defects – latent defects	10 years	Substantial completion – the later of final building inspection, notice of completion is issued; or certificate of occupancy is issued.	Maximum of 10 years (additional 2 years granted if defect is discovered in final year).	Nev. Rev. Stat. § 11.202
New Hampshire	Construction defects	8 years	Substantial completion of construction		N.H. Rev. Stat. Ann. § 508:4-b

State	Type of Action	Period of Repose	Commencement	Comment	State Code Section
New Jersey	Construction defects	10 years	Performance or furnishing of services and construction		N.J. Stat. Ann. § 2A:14-1.1
New Mexico	Construction defects	10 years	Substantial completion of construction		N.M. Stat. Ann. § 37-1-27
New York	Construction defects	6 years	Completion of construction	For construction contracts litigation involving defective construction, the date of completion accrual rule applies not only to the contracting parties but also to those with a relationship amounting to the "functional equivalent of privity." *City School Dist. Of the City of Newburgh v. Hugh Stubbins & Assocs., Inc.,* 650 N.E.2d 399, 401 (N.Y. App. Civ. 1995); *Town of W. Seneca v. Kidney Architects, P.C.,* 187 A.D.3d 1509 (N.Y. App. 2020).	N.Y.C.P.L.R. § 213
North Carolina	Construction defects	6 years	Later of last act or omission giving rise to cause of action or substantial completion of construction		N.C. Gen. Stat. § 1-50(a)(5)
North Dakota	Construction defects	10 years	Substantial completion of construction	Maximum of 12 years (additional 2 years granted if defect is discovered in final year).	N.D. Cent. Code, § 28-01-44
Ohio	Construction defects	10 years	Substantial completion of construction	Maximum of 12 years (additional 2 years granted if defect is discovered in final 2 years).	Ohio Rev. Code. Ann. § 2305.131
Oklahoma	Construction defects	10 years	Substantial completion of construction	Does not apply to contract actions.	Okla. Stat. tit. 12, § 109
Oregon	Construction defects	10 years	Substantial completion or abandonment	6 years for large commercial structures	Or. Rev. Stat. § 12.135

State	Type of Action	Period of Repose	Commencement	Comment	State Code Section
Pennsylvania	Construction defects	12 years	Completion of construction	Maximum of 14 years (additional 2 years granted if defect is discovered in final 2 years).	42 Pa. Cons. Stat. § 5536
Rhode Island	Construction defects – contracts and implied warranty	10 years	When evidence of injury to property is or should be significant enough to alert the injured. *Lee v. Morin,* 469 A.2d 358, 360 (R.I. 1983).	This is a statute of limitations not repose.	R.I. Gen. Laws § 9-1-13(a); *Boghossian v. Ferland Corp.,* 600 A.2d 288 (R.I. 1991).
	Construction defects – torts	10 years	Substantial completion of construction		R.I. Gen. Laws § 9-1-29
South Carolina	Construction defects	8 years	Substantial completion of construction		S.C. Code Ann. § 15-3-640
South Dakota	Construction defects	10 years	Substantial completion of construction		S.D. Codified Laws § 15-2A-3
Tennessee	Construction defects	4 years	Substantial completion of construction	Maximum of 5 years (additional year granted if defect is discovered in final year).	Tenn. Code Ann. §§ 28-3-202 and 28-3-203
Texas	Construction defects	10 years*	Substantial completion of construction	Maximum of 12 years (additional 2 years granted if defect is discovered in final year). *This period is reduced to 6 years if the person being sued is a contractor who has provided a written warranty for the residence that offers 1 year for workmanship and materials; 2 years for plumbing, electrical, heating, and air-conditioning delivery systems; and 6 years for major structural components.	Tex. Civ. Prac. & Rem. Code Ann. § 16.009

State	Type of Action	Period of Repose	Commencement	Comment	State Code Section
Utah	Construction defects—contract and warranty	6 years	Completion or abandonment of construction		Utah Code Ann. § 78B-2-309
	Construction defects—other than contract and warranty	9 years	Completion or abandonment of construction	Maximum of 11 years (additional 2 years granted if defect is discovered in final 2 years).	Utah Code Ann. § 78B-2-225.
Vermont	Civil actions	6 years	After the cause of action accrues	*See Union Sch. Dist. V. Lench,* 134 Vt. 424 (Vt. 1976) (stating that there is no discovery rule).	Vt. Stat. Ann. Tit. 12, § 511
Virginia	Construction defects	5 years	Performance or furnishing of services and construction		Va. Code Ann. § 8.01-250; *see, also,* Va. Code Ann. § 55.1-357 which creates statutory warranties of 1 year for structural defects, workmanship and habitability and 5 years for foundations and also provides that suits must be brought within 2 years of a breach of warranty.
Washington	Construction defects	6 years	Later of substantial completion of construction or termination of services		Wash. Rev. Code § 4.16.310
West Virginia	Construction defects	10 years	Performance or furnishing of services and construction		W. Va. Code § 55-2-6a
Wisconsin	Construction defects	7 years	Substantial completion of construction	Maximum of 10 years (additional 3 years granted if defect is discovered in final 3 years).	Wis. Stat. § 893.89
Wyoming	Construction defects	10 years	Substantial completion of construction	Maximum of 11 years (additional year granted if defect is discovered in final year).	Wyo. Stat. Ann. § 1-3-111

Cases and Statutes, State by State

Cases and Statutes Involving New Home Construction Warranties and Contracts

This appendix includes sample cases in those states that have addressed the doctrine of implied warranty in a new home construction context. In those states where no entry appears, we determined that the courts in those states had not adequately addressed the issue for the purposes of this publication. The authors have attempted to exclude cases related to remodeling because the warranties applied to remodeling often differ from those for new home construction.

In a few instances, the authors refer to unpublished court opinions to illustrate a legal point. Unpublished court opinions do not have legal precedent (weight), and therefore, they suggest that you not rely on these cases in legal briefs. Use caution when referring to unpublished court opinions and check your local court rules before citing to such decisions.

Case law citations are current as of the date of publication. Please be advised that case law changes through new case decisions or statutory enactments. Builders and remodelers should consult with their local attorney for information concerning the current status of the law in their jurisdiction.

Alabama

Alabama courts recognize an implied warranty of fitness and habitability in the sale of a home newly constructed by a builder. *Sims v. Lewis*, 374 So. 2d 298 (Ala. 1979) (adopting implied warranty of habitability for "situations involving the sale of a new house by a builder-vendor"). Therefore, the rule of *caveat emptor* (let the buyer beware) no longer applies to such a sale. *Turner v. Westhampton Court, L.L.C.*, 903 So. 2d 82, 92 (Ala. 2004) (affirming *Cochran v. Keeton*, 252 So. 2d 313 (Ala. 1971)).

See generally, *Blackmon v. Powell*, 132 So. 3d 1 (Ala. 2013) (" . . . we hold that the Blackmons failed to put forth any evidence indicating that Powell did not perform his work with reasonable or ordinary skill. The trial court therefore properly entered a summary judgment in favor of Powell on the breach-of-contract and breach-of-implied-warranty-of-workmanship claims). The sale of a used home in Alabama is still governed by the doctrine of *caveat emptor*, and there is no implied warranty of habitability. *Boakle v. Bedwell Constr., Inc.* 770 So. 2d 1076 (Ala. 2000).

However, Alabama does recognize that the parties can agree to disclaim the implied warranty of habitability. *Turner*, 903 So. 2d at 92. In *Turner*, the court stated, "the principle of freedom of contract permits a party to effectively disclaim the implied warranty of habitability." *Id.* When real estate is "new," it carries with it the implied warranty of habitability. *Cruse v. Coldwell Banker/Graben Real Estate Inc.*, 667 So. 2d 714 (Ala. 1995). *Caveat emptor* still applies to the sale of a used home. *Boackle v. Bedwell Constr. Co., Inc.*, 770 So. 2d 1076, 1079 (Ala. 2000). Alabama does not extend implied warranties to the sale of a "used" home. *Boackle*, 770 So. 2d at 1079.

Implied warranties apply to a defective retaining wall (*Briggs v. Woodfin*, 388 So. 2d 1221 (Ala. Civ. App. 1980)) and a defective septic system (*Sims v. Lewis*, 374 So. 2d 298 (Ma. 1979)), but they do not apply to the purchase of land (*Morris v. Strickling*, 579 So. 2d 609, 610–11 (Ala. 1991); *Scott v. Gill*, 352 So. 2d 1143 (Ala. Civ. App. 1977)). Implied warranties do not extend to subsequent purchasers. *Cooper & Co. v. Bryant*, 440 So. 2d 1016 (Ala. 1983).

Emotional distress damages might be recoverable by the purchaser in a breach of warranty action against the builder. *B & M Homes, Inc. v. Hogan*, 376 So. 2d 667 (Ala. 1979).

Warranty claims are subject to a two-year statute of limitations and a seven-year statute of repose. An action against an architect, engineer, or builder "shall be commenced within two years next after a cause of action accrues or arises, and not thereafter." Ala. Code § 6-5-221. Notwithstanding the foregoing, no relief can be granted on any cause of action which accrues or would have accrued more than seven years after the substantial completion of construction of the improvement on or to the real property, and any right of action which accrues or would have accrued more than seven years thereafter is barred, except where prior to the expiration of such seven-year period, the architect, engineer, or builder had actual knowledge that such defect or deficiency exists and failed to disclose such defect or deficiency to the person with whom the architect, engineer, or builder contracted to perform such service. Ala. Code § 6-5-221.

In *Stephens v. Creel*, 429 So. 2d 278 (Ala. 1983), the court was faced with the question whether the statute of limitations for a construction warranty claim began to run (1) when the construction contract was entered into, (2) when the contract was breached, or (3) when damage to the house was discovered. 429 So. 2d at 279. The court chose the second option: "The statute of limitations does not begin to run upon the entering into of a contract, but when the contract is breached, and a cause of action accrues." 429 So. 2d at 280. In a contract action based upon a warranty to construct a house in a workmanlike manner, the cause of action accrues, and the statute of limitations begins to run on the date the defendant completes performance. By its very nature it is the failure to *construct* the house in a workmanlike manner that constitutes the breach. *See also, Beasley v. 500 Finishes Corp.*, 2018 WL 3848815 at *8 (M.D. Ala. August 13, 2018) (rejecting the builder's argument that because it did not complete the house that the action did not accrue).

Alaska

In building or construction contracts, whenever someone holds him or herself out to be specially qualified to do a particular type of work, an implied warranty guarantees that the builder or contractor will perform the work in a workmanlike manner and that the resulting building will be reasonably fit for its intended use. *Lewis v. Anchorage Asphalt Paving Co.*, 535 P.2d 1188 (Alaska 1975); *Davis v. McCall*, 568 P.2d 956 (Alaska 1977) (In an action by homeowners against a building contractor for breach of a remodeling contract, there was evidence that a cabinetmaker, a building inspector, and an appraiser considered Davis' work to be well below the ordinary standards of the trade); *John's Heating Serv. v. Lamb*, 46 P.3d 1024, 1037 (Alaska 2002). A small-volume subdivider was not liable for breach of warranty when he innocently failed to disclose undetected permafrost conditions in lots sold to the purchasers. *Stephanov v. Gavrilovich*, 594 P.2d 30 (Alaska 1979).

When providing plans and specifications to a contractor, an owner makes an implied warranty that they will be sufficient for their particular purpose. If the defective specifications cause the contractor to incur extra costs in performing the contract, then the contractor may recover his costs stemming from the breach of implied warranty. *Alaska v. Transamerica Premier Ins. Co.*, 856 P.2d 766 (Alaska 1993).

Arizona

Arizona implies a warranty of workmanship and habitability in every contract entered between a builder-vendor and a homebuyer. *See Zambrano v. M & RC II LLC*, 517 P.3d 1168 (Ariz. 2022). *See also Columbia Western*

Corp. v. Vela, 592 P.2d 1294 (Ariz. 1979). The purpose of an implied warranty of workmanship and habitability is to protect innocent purchasers and to hold builders accountable for their work. *Richards v. Powercraft Homes, Inc.*, 678 P.2d 427 (Ariz. 1984). Under the warranty, the home must be reasonably suited for its intended purpose and not simply habitable. *Nastri v. Wood Bros. Homes, Inc.*, 690 P.2d 158 (Ariz. Ct. App. 1984). The standard for determining whether a breach has occurred is one of reasonableness in light of the surrounding circumstances (age of the house, its maintenance, "the use to which it has been put"). *Richards*, 678 P.2d at 430. The implied warranties are limited to latent defects that would not have been discoverable had a reasonable inspection been made prior to the purchase. A reasonable inspection does not require an inspection by an expert or professional home inspection service; rather, an implied warranty does not extend to defects that the average purchaser could have discovered. *Hershey v. Rich Rosen Constr. Co.*, 81 P.2d 55 (Ariz. Ct. App. 1991).

Furthermore, the "implied warranty of habitability and proper workmanship is not unlimited." *Richards*, 678 P.2d at 430. It does not require the builder-vendor to "act as an insurer for subsequent vendees" as the court in *Richards* feared. *Id.* The implied warranty is limited to latent defects that become manifest after the subsequent owner's purchase and that were not discoverable had a reasonable inspection of the structure been made prior to the purchase. *Hayden Bus. Ctr. Condo. Ass'n v. Pegasus Dev. Corp.*, 105 P.3d 157, 159 (Ariz. Ct. App. 2005) (citing *Richards v. Powercraft*, 678 P.2d 427). *See also Maycock v. Asilomar Dev. Inc.*, 88 P.3d 565, 570 (Ariz. Ct. App. 2004) (limiting the implied warranty to "latent defects which become manifest after the subsequent owner's purchase, and which were not discoverable had a reasonable inspection of the structure been made prior to purchase").

Arizona courts apply the implied warranty, which extends to subsequent purchasers, to structural defects (*Woodward v. Chirco Constr. Co.*, 687 P.2d 1269 (Ariz. 1984)); faulty stucco application (*Hershey*, 817 P.2d at 60–61); and latent defects in the construction relating to soil compaction (*Nastri*, 690 P.2d at 159). However, the implied warranty did not apply to termite protection where 13 years passed from construction to discovery of the damage because the soil treatment for termites is expected to last no longer than five years. *Sheibels v. Estes Homes*, 778 P.2d 1299 (Ariz. 1989). In *Yanni v. Tucker Plumbing*, 312 P.3d 1130 (Ariz. Ct. App. 2013), the court held that lack of contractual privity precluded homeowners from asserting claims against subcontractors for breach of warranty of workmanship and habitability.

Different parts of construction may have different life expectancies, such as a foundation compared to a roof. In addition, the duration of an implied warranty depends, in part, on the life expectancy of the questioned component in a non-defective condition. *Hershey,* 81 P.2d 55; *see also Sheibels,* 778 P.2d 1299. For an innocent subsequent purchaser, an express warranty for a limited time cannot displace the implied warranties, and a disclaimer of the implied warranties in the original purchaser's contract is voided by public policy regarding an innocent subsequent purchaser. *Nastri,* 690 P.2d at 161.

In *Zambrano,* the court concluded that the public policy underlying the implied warranty of workmanship and habitability precluded the parties from disclaiming and waiving it, and it went on to find that "unless the legislature enacts a statute permitting waiver of the implied warranty, our courts will not permit it." *Zambrano,* 517 P.3d at 1179.

The statute of repose is not limited to claims brought by property owners, but also bars claims among the construction and design professionals involved in the construction, and thus was properly applied in this case to bar a contractor's breach of contract and warranty claims against one of its subcontractors. *Evans Withycombe, Inc. v. Western Innovations, Inc.,* 159 P.3d 547 (Ariz. Ct. App. 2006).

Arkansas

An implied warranty of habitability by a builder-vendor goes with the sale of new housing. The implied warranty guarantees that the builder-vendor built the structure in a good and workmanlike manner and that the structure is fit for human habitation. *Coney v. Stewart,* 562 S.W.2d 619 (Ark. 1978); *Wawak v. Stewart,* 449 S.W.2d 922 (Ark. 1970). The implied warranty of fitness and habitability also exists when a builder constructs a new residence with plans supplied by the purchaser. *Daniel v. Quick,* 606 S.W.2d 81 (Ark. Ct. App. 1980). The Arkansas Supreme Court held there is an implied warranty of fitness and habitability in the sale of a new house by a seller who is also the builder. *Curry v. Thornsberry,* 128 S.W.3d 438, 444 (Ark. 2003).

The implied warranty "does not rest on an agreement in fact but is imposed by law as a matter of public policy to promote fairness." *Wingfield v. Page,* 644 S.W.2d 940 (Ark. 1983). Implied warranties extend for a reasonable period to subsequent purchasers for latent defects not discoverable upon reasonable inspection. *Blagg v. Fred Hunt Co., Inc.,* 612 S.W.2d 321 (Ark. 1981); *see also Curry,* 128 S.W.3d at 444 (extending implied warranties to subsequent purchasers). Implied warranties extend to all integral parts and systems of the house where the breakdown relates to its design or installation. *Pickler v. Fisher,* 644 S.W.2d 644, 645 (Ark. Ct. App. 1983). Courts have applied implied warranties to (a) a defect arising from a failure to utilize the proper foundation for existing soils (*Wingfield*, 644 S.W.2d 940), (b) a septic system tank and drain field system (*Coney*, 562 S.W.2d 619), and (c) faulty brickwork (*Carter v. Quick*, 563 S.W.2d 461 (Ark. 1978)). Causation is not an element of a claim for breach of contract or breach of implied warranty of habitability. *Crumpacker v. Gary Reed Const., Inc.* 374 S.W.3d 162 (Ark. Ct. App. 2010) (Here, the Crumpackers presented evidence that the house that Reed built was defective. They also presented evidence that they sustained monetary damages as a result of those defects. Nothing more was required of them to withstand a motion for summary judgment). And the purchaser of the home need not list each and every objection, but the purchaser must clearly tell the builder that the purchaser believes a breach of warranty has occurred and give the builder sufficient opportunity to inspect the premises and correct the defects. *Pickler*, 644 S.W.2d at 646. The law also provides that a contractor who built a new dwelling be entitled to at least some notice of defects in a breach of warranty action, despite the fact that the Uniform Commercial Code does not govern the transaction. *Cinnamon Valley Resort v. EMAC Enters.*, 202 S.W.3d 1 (Ark. Ct. App. 2005); *Pennington v. Rhodes*, 929 S.W.2d 169 (Ark. Ct. App. 1996). In *Pennington*, the court declined to hold that a purchaser of a newly built dwelling is required to list every defect of construction in order to preserve a breach of warranty claim. *Pennington*, 929 S.W.2d at 172. Instead, the court held "notification need only be with sufficient clarity to apprise the vendor-builder that a breach of warranty is being asserted and to give him sufficient opportunity to inspect the premises and correct the defects." *Id*. at 172–73.

A builder may exclude implied warranties when the circumstances surrounding the transaction are in themselves sufficient to call the buyer's attention to the fact that the builder made no implied warranties or that the builder excluded a certain implied warranty. *O'Mara v. Dykema*, 942 S.W.2d 854 (Ark. 1997); *Wingfield*, 644 S.W.2d 940; *Carter*, 563 S.W.2d 461. *But see Bullington v. Palangio*, 45 S.W.3d 834 (Ark. 2001) (The implied warranties of habitability and proper construction were not waived because they were not included in the language of the express warranty on workmanship).

When an owner supplies plans and specifications to a contractor, an implied warranty arises that these are adequate and suitable. *Graham Constr. Co. v. Earl*, 208 S.W.3d 106 (Ark. 2005). In *Graham*, the court held the owner liable to the contractor "for damages resulting from faulty plans and specifications." *Id*. The court determined that the stipulation requiring the contractor to conduct on-site inspections and examine the plans and specifications did not nullify the implied warranty. *Id*. Nevertheless, the court did note "a competent and experienced contractor cannot rely upon submitted specifications and plans where he is fully aware, or should have been aware, that the plans and specifications cannot produce the proposed results. Therefore, where delays result, as here, because of faulty specifications and plans, the owner will have to respond in damages for the resulting additional expenses realized by the contractor." *Id.*

California

Builders and sellers of new construction are subject to the implied warranty that such structures have been designed and built in a reasonably workmanlike manner. *Pollard v. Saxe & Yolles Dev. Co.,* 525 P.2d 88 (Cal. 1974); *see also Siders v. Schloo,* 233 Cal. Rptr. 906 (1987); *East Hilton Drive Homeowners' Ass'n v. Western Real Estate Exchange, Inc.,* 186 Cal. Rptr. 267 (1982). In California, the "general rule is that privity of contract [between the plaintiff and defendant] is required in an action for breach of either express or implied warranty and that there is no privity between the original seller and a subsequent purchaser who is [not] a party to the original sale." *Windham at Carmel Mountain Ranch Ass'n v. Superior Court,* 109 Cal. App. 4th 1162, 1169 (Cal. Ct. App. 2003). Furthermore, the court in *Windham* found that "builders and sellers of new construction should be held to what is impliedly represented—that the completed structure was designed and constructed in a reasonably workmanlike manner." *Windham,* 109 Cal. App. 4th at 1169 (citing *Pollard,* 525 P.2d 88).

The buyer is required to give notice of breach of warranty within a reasonable time after he or she discovers or should have discovered the breach. *Pollard,* 525 P.2d 88. Civ. Code, §§ 895–945.5 (commonly known as the Right to Repair Act) sets forth detailed statewide standards that the components of a dwelling must satisfy. It also establishes a prelitigation dispute resolution process that affords builders notice of alleged construction defects and the opportunity to cure such defects, while granting homeowners the right to sue for deficiencies even in the absence of property damage or personal injury. The Act added title 7 to division 2, part 2 of the Civil Code. (§§ 895–945.5.) That title consists of five chapters. Chapter 1 establishes definitions applicable to the entire title. (§ 895.) Chapter 2 defines standards for building construction. (§§ 896–897.) Chapter 3 governs various builder obligations, including the warranties a builder must provide. (§§ 900–907.) Chapter 4 creates a prelitigation dispute resolution process. (§§ 910–938.) Chapter 5 describes the procedures for lawsuits under the Act. (§§ 941–945.5.) *See McMillin Albany, LLC v. Superior Court,* 408 P.3d 797 (Cal. 2018). Although the Legislature preserved common law claims for personal injury, it made the Act the virtually exclusive remedy not just for economic loss but also for property damage arising from construction defects. *McMillin,* 408 P.3d at 799.

In the present case, we are asked to determine whether homeowners may bring a class action asserting a claim under the Act against the manufacturer of an allegedly defective plumbing fixture used in the construction of class members' homes. Based on our examination of the structure and language of the Act, as well as the legislative history, we conclude that class actions are not allowed under the Act except in one limited context: to assert claims that address solely the incorporation into a residence of a defective component, unless that component is a product that is completely manufactured offsite. *Kohler v. Superior Court*, 29 Cal.App.5th 55, 240 Cal.Rptr.3d 426 (2018) (Because the claim in this case involves allegedly defective products that were completely manufactured offsite, we hold that the claim alleged under the Act cannot be litigated as a class action).

River's Side at Washington Square Homeowners Association, which was created to manage a development consisting of 25 residential units and one commercial unit, each of which was separately owned by River's Side's members, sued the developers and others for "defects in the structures, components, and common areas" of the development. The court held that, where the HOA's cause of action was expressly brought pursuant to the Right to Repair Act, it did not have standing because the claim related only to defects in individual units. However, the HOA had standing to bring claims against vendors of individual units for breach of contract, nondisclosure, and misrepresentation, which were not subject to Right to Repair law, as to defects in common areas. *See River's Side at Washington Square Homeowners Ass'n v. The Superior Court of Yolo County*, 88 Cal.App.5th 1209, 305 Cal.Rptr.3d 532 (2023).

Colorado

The contractual responsibilities of the builder of a new house that are implicit in the concept of "implied warranty of habitability" include the buyer's right to both a home that is built in a workmanlike manner and one that is suitable for habitation. *Roper v. Spring Lake Dev. Co.*, 789 P.2d 483 (Colo. Ct. App. 1990); *see also Carpenter v. Donohoe*, 388 P.2d 399 (Colo. 1964). *See Hildebrand v. New Vista Homes II, LLC.*, 252 P.3d 1159, 1169 (Colo. 2010) (likening the breach of an implied warranty claim to strict liability for construction defects). The question of the existence of a warranty and whether that warranty was breached is ordinarily one for the trier of fact. *Stroh v. Am. Recreation & Mobile Home Corp. of Colo.*, 530 P.2d 989, 993 (Colo. Ct. App. 1975). Whether an Association may bring implied warranty claims for defects in the common areas on behalf of its members is a question of law. *Brooktree Homeowners Ass'n v. Brooktree Village, LLC.*, 479 P.3d 86 (Colo. Ct. App. 2020).

The implied warranties of workmanlike manner and habitability extend to a house in the process of construction. *Mulhern v. Hederich,* 430 P.2d 469 (Colo. 1967). The implied warranties apply even when the builder constructs the house for his personal use and later sells it to a member of the general public. *Sloat v. Matheny,* 625 P.2d 1031,1033 (Colo. 1981). A home buyer may not pursue a claim against a developer for a breach of implied warranty of suitability where there is no contractual privity between the home buyer and the developer. *Forest City Stapleton, Inc. v. Rogers,* 393 P.3d 487 (Colo. 2017).

To establish liability under an implied warranty a homeowner must prove that the defect was a result of improper construction, design, or preparation. *Cosmopolitan Homes, Inc, v. Weller,* 663 P.2d 1041 (Colo. 1983). A builder has a duty to use reasonable care and skill in construction of a home, and the failure to do so constitutes negligence. *Hoang v. Arbess,* 80 P.3d 863, 867 (Colo. Ct. App. 2003) (citing *Cosmopolitan Homes Inc. v. Weller,* 663 P.2d 1041, 1042–1043 (Colo. 1983)) (noting "[a]n obligation to act without negligence in the construction of a home is independent of contractual obligations such as an implied warranty of habitability . . . A contractual obligation gives rise to a common law duty to perform the work subject to the contract with reasonable care and skill"). When a developer improves and sells land, for the express purpose of residential construction, to a purchaser who relies on the developer's expertise, an implied representation arises that the property is suitable for the residential purpose for which it is sold, *i.e.*, habitation. *Beeftu v. Creekside Ventures LLC,* 37 P.3d 526, 528 (Colo. Ct. App. 2001).

A builder is not required to build a perfect house; the test is reasonableness in terms of what the workman of average skill and intelligence would ordinarily do. *Shiffers v. Cunningham Shepherd Builders, Co.,* 470 P.2d 593 (Colo. Ct. App. 1970). The implied warranty applies where the builder fails to comply with local building codes (*Carpenter,* 388 P.2d 399), and it applies when defective drainage around the house results in vertical displacement of the driveway (*Belt v. Spencer,* 585 P.2d 922 (Colo. Ct. App. 1978)). The implied warranty extends to cracks in the exterior surface of the house as well as the water supply. *Glisan v. Smolenske,* 387 P.2d 260 (Colo. 1963); *Mazurek v. Nielsen,* 599 P.2d 269 (Colo. Ct. App. 1979). The implied warranty of habitability is limited to the first purchasers. *Gillespie v. Plemmons,* 849 P.2d 838 (Colo. Ct. App. 1992); *see also Brooktree Homeowners Ass'n,* 479 P.3d at 94 ("Because only persons in privity of contract with a builder or seller have implied warranties, the class of purchasers entitled to the protection of an implied warranty is limited to first purchasers. Subsequent purchasers are not in privity with the builder or seller and, for this reason, cannot assert implied warranty claims.") (internal citations omitted). A builder may limit the implied warranties if the builder states in the contract the limitation in clear and unambiguous language. *Sloat v. Matheny*, 625 P.2d at 1034.

In 2007, the Colorado Legislature extended further protection to residential property owners by passing the Homeowner Protection Act of 2007 (HPA). Prior to the enactment of the HPA, builders and developers were able to disclaim implied warranties so long as the language in the purchase and sale agreement was clear, unambiguous, and sufficiently particular to provide adequate notice of the implied warranty protections that were being relinquished. The HPA makes void as against public policy any disclaimer of implied warranty or any other waiver or limitation of a legal right afforded to homeowners under the Construction Defect Action Reform Act. The HPA applies to cases filed on or after April 20, 2007. However, any waiver or limitation between the residential property owner and a construction professional after a claim has accrued is not void under this same section. *See* C.R.S.A. § 13-20-806. *See also Broomfield Senior Living Owner, LLC v. R.G. Brinkmann Company*, 413 P.3d 219 (Colo. Ct. App. 2017) (a senior assisted and independent living facility constituted a "residential property" under the Colorado Construction Defect Action Reform Act and therefore was included within the protections provided by the Homeowner Protection Act).

Connecticut

Connecticut statutes provide for express and implied warranties in the sale of new homes and conversion condominiums. Conn. Gen. Stat. Ann. §§ 47-116 to 121 (New Home Warranty Act or NHWA); § 47-74 (e). Under § 47-116 of the NHWA, express warranties pursuant to § 47-117 can only be created by a "vendor" and only run to a "purchaser." The statute defines a purchaser as "the original buyer, his heirs or designated representatives, of any improved real estate." Conn. Gen. Stat. Ann. § 47- 116. A vendor means "any person engaged in the business of erecting or creating an improvement on real estate, any declarant of a conversion condominium, or any person to whom a completed improvement has been granted for resale in the course of his business." *Id.*

The NHWA is a remedial, consumer protection statute "that must be liberally construed in favor of purchasers and strictly against sellers. *But see Middlesex Mut. Assur. Co. v. Lemon Builders*, 2007 WL 3380462 (Conn. Sup. Ct., Oct. 31, 2007) (The plaintiff cites no Connecticut case, nor does the court's research find any case law, which would indicate that both a common-law warranty and the statutory warranties of §§ 47 116 through 47-121 apply to a scenario such as the present one. This court will not adopt an additional common-law warranty of habitability and good workmanship based solely on the law of another jurisdiction). *See also Amica Mutual Ins. Co. v. Abar Development, LLC*, 2013 WL 1800453 (Conn. Super. Ct., April 3, 2013) ("The parties do not provide, and the court does not find, a Connecticut case that recognizes an independent common-law cause of action for breach of implied warranty absent allegations of a breach of contract.").

In an action alleging violations under the New Home Warranty Act, the trial court's damages award was clearly erroneous because of its failure to award the plaintiffs damages adequate to pay for the labor necessary to replace the trim and siding, as well as to repair and repaint damaged portions of the home's interior. *See Naples v. Keystone Bldg. and Dev. Corp.*, 990 A.2d 326 (Conn. 2010).

Express warranties may be created as to (a) written facts or promises that relate to the improvement (an improvement is anything that enhances the value of the property permanently, such as a building or a fence) and that are made a part of the parties' agreement; (b) any written description of the improvement, including plans and specifications that are made a part of the parties' agreement; and (c) any sample or model that is made a part of the basis of the bargain between the builder and the purchaser. Conn. Gen. Stat. Ann. § 47-117(a). No formal words such as guarantee, or warranty shall be necessary to create an express warranty. Conn. Gen. Stat. Ann. § 47-117(b). An express warranty shall terminate: "(1) In the case of an improvement completed at the time of the delivery of the deed to the purchaser, one year after the delivery or one year after the taking of possession by the purchaser, whichever occurs first; and (2) in the case of an improvement not completed at the time of delivery of the deed to the purchaser, one year after the date of the completion or one year after taking of possession by the purchaser, whichever occurs first." Conn. Gen. Stat. Ann. § 47-117(d).

In every sale of an improvement by a builder to a purchaser, warranties are implied that the improvement is (a) free from faulty materials, (b) constructed according to sound engineering standards, (c) constructed in a workmanlike manner, and (d) fit for habitation. Conn. Gen. Stat. Ann. § 47-118(a). Implicit in a building contract for the construction of a dwelling is a promise by the builder that he or she will complete the house in a skillful, competent, and workmanlike manner. Conn. Gen. Stat. Ann. § 47-118(a). The warranties do not apply to any condition that an inspection of the premises would reveal to a reasonably diligent purchaser at the time the parties sign the contract. Conn. Gen. Stat. Ann. § 47 118(b). However, the statutory implied warranties apply to both the newly constructed single-family dwelling and the lot upon which it sits when sold to a purchaser as a package by the builder-vendor. *Krawiec v. Blake Manor Dev. Corp.*, 602 A.2d 1062 (Conn. 1992). The implied warranties shall terminate after 1 year. Conn. Gen. Stat. Ann. § 47-118(e). The 1-year period is a limitation upon the period within which an action for breach of warranty may arise, not within which it must commence. *Cashman v. Calvo*, 493 A.2d 891 (Conn. 1985). The parties can waive the implied warranties if they do so according to the terms of the statute. Conn. Gen. Stat. Ann. § 47-118(d).

The issuance by the building department of any municipality of a certificate of occupancy for any newly constructed single-family dwelling shall carry an implied warranty that the builder has complied with the building code or the customary application and interpretation of the building code of such municipality. Any action brought for breach of the warranty must commence within three years from the date of the issuance of the certificate of occupancy. Conn. Gen. Stat. Ann. § 47-121.

A contractor incurs no liability resulting from defective plans provided by the contractee. *D'Esopo & Co. v. Bleiler*, 538 A.2d 719 (Conn. Ct. App. 1988); *see also Southern New England Contracting Co. v. State*, 345 A.2d 550 (Conn. 1974).

Conn. Gen. Stat. Ann. § 47-117 "expressly provides that no words in the contract of sale shall work to exclude or to modify any warranties created under the statutes unless there is a separate agreement on exclusion or modification." To the extent that a provision in the sales contract modified the express warranty provision in §47-117(d) it "was inoperative because the modification was not the subject of a written instrument signed by the purchaser after the original contract was executed." *Beucler v. Lloyd*, 851 A.2d 358 (Conn. Ct. App. 2004).

Delaware

Delaware recognizes an implied warranty of good quality and workmanship in the builder's construction of a new home. *Smith v. Berwin Builders, Inc.*, 287 A.2d 693 (Del. 1972). *See Lee-Scott v. Shute*, 2017 WL 1201158 (Del. Com. Pl., January 30, 2017) (Under the Implied Warranty of Good Quality and Workmanship, contractors involved in building homes or home additions must have the appropriate skill to "perform the work they offer . . . 'in a skillful and workmanlike manner.'") (citations omitted).

Its implied warranty of habitability is not distinct from the warranty of good quality and workmanship. *Council of Unit Owners of Breakwater House Condo. v. Simpler*, 603 A.2d 792, 795 (Del. 1992). In *Council of Unit Owners*, the court noted, "Habitability may be a component of good workmanship where the contract involves a residence, but there is no support in Delaware law for the existence of an implied warranty of habitability as such." *Id.* at 795. "[A]n otherwise existing implied warranty of good quality and workmanship will not be defeated merely because the contract to which it applies is one involving substantial renovation by a developer rather than completely new construction performed by a builder." *Id.* at 796. In a particular case, a developer who would otherwise be subject to an implied warranty of good quality and workmanship cannot escape that warranty merely by arranging for the actual construction to be performed by a contractual agent, the builder. *Council of Unit Owners*, 603 A.2d at 796. The Superior Court held that a company that subcontracted to install stucco on the exterior of the house addition was bound by the implied warranty of good quality and workmanship. *Casale Constr., LLC. v. Best Stucco, LLC*, 2014 WL 1316150 (Del. Super., March 28, 2014).

District of Columbia

"Modern contract law has recognized that the buyer of goods and services in an industrialized society must rely upon the skill and honesty of the supplier to assure that goods and services purchased are of adequate quality[.]" *Javins v. First National Realty Corp.*, 428 F.2d 1071 (D.C. Cir. 1970). Courts have "steadily widened the seller's responsibility for the quality of goods and services through implied warranties of fitness and merchantability." *Id.* at 1075. "Today most states as well as the District of Columbia have codified and enacted these warranties into statute, as to the sale of goods, in the Uniform Commercial Code." *Id.* Further, the court in *Javins* stated that "Implied warranties of quality have not been limited to cases involving sales." *Id.* at 1075. The court recognized that "courts have begun to hold sellers and developers of real property responsible for the quality of their product" giving as examples that "builders of new homes have recently been held liable to purchasers for improper construction on the grounds that the builders had breached an implied warranty of fitness." *Id.* at 1076.

Florida

Florida courts have rejected the doctrine of *caveat emptor* (buyer beware) in favor of the doctrine of implied warranty. Those courts have held that a builder-vendor of a new home impliedly warrants that the home is habitable and that the home is built in a workmanlike manner. *See Conklin v. Hurley*, 428 So. 2d 654 (Fla. 1983); *Gable v. Silver*, 258 So. 2d 11 (Fla. 1972); *West Florida Community Builders, Inc. v. Mitchell*, 528 So. 2d 979 (Fla. Ct. App. 1988); *Hesson v. Walmsley Constr. Co.*, 422 So. 2d 943 (Fla. Ct. App. 1982); *Burger v. Hector*, 278 So. 2d 636 (Fla. Ct. App. 1973). The rationale of the cases that relax or abandon the doctrine of *caveat emptor* is that the purchaser is not in an equal bargaining position with the builder-vendor of a new dwelling, and the purchaser is forced to rely upon the skill and knowledge of the builder-vendor with respect to the materials and workmanship of an adequately constructed dwelling house. *Conklin,* 428 So. 2d at 657.

"The test for a breach of implied warranty is whether the premises meet ordinary, normal standards reasonably to be expected of living quarters of comparable kind and quality." *Hesson,* 422 So. 2d at 945. An implied warranty extends only to conditions in existence at the time of the sale to avoid unfairly holding a builder-vendor liable for defects caused by conditions occurring subsequent to sale, e.g., natural catastrophes, such as earth tremors and sinkholes. *West Florida Community Builders, Inc. v. Mitchell,* 528 So. 2d 979 (citing *Hesson,* 422 So. 2d at 945). Moreover, the warranty does not extend to the sale of unimproved lots. *See Schmitt v. Long,* 290 So. 2d 139 (Fla. Ct. App. 1974). The soil was not suitable for the laying of the foundation of the house without extensive demucking and compacting. In *Conklin,* the court held that implied warranties of fitness and merchantability do not extend to first purchasers of unimproved residential real estate. *Conklin,* 428 So. 2d at 658. Implied warranties of fitness for a particular purpose, habitability, and merchantability apply to structures in common areas of a subdivision that immediately support the residence in the form of essential services. *Lakeview Reserve Homeowners v. Maronda Homes, Inc.,* 48 So. 3d 902 (Fla. Dist. Ct. App. 2010) (*aff'd,* 127 So. 3d 1258 (Fla. 2013)) (roads, drainage systems, retention ponds and underground pipes were deemed essential). The HOA has the legal right to institute an action on behalf of its members for matters that concern the members' common interest. *Maronda Homes, Inc. of Florida v. Lakeview Reserve Homeowners Ass'n, Inc.,* 127 So. 3d 1258, 1268 (Fla. 2013).

During the pendency of *Maronda Homes, Inc. of Florida v. Lakeview Reserve Homeowners Ass'n, Inc.,* the Florida Legislature enacted section 553.835, Florida Statutes (2012). Pursuant to Section 553.835(4), "There is no cause of action in law or equity to a purchaser of a home or to a homeowners association based upon the doctrine or theory of implied warranty of fitness and merchantability or habitability for damages to *off-site improvements.*" (emphasis added). Thus, under Section 553.835, for an individual to have a cause of action for breach of the implied warranties, he must establish that (1) the claim is regarding a new home, (2) the claim is with regard to damage to the home or a structure or improvement on or under the home's lot, *and* (3) the complained of improvement or structure immediately and directly supports the habitability of the home.

In Florida, certain statutory warranties apply to condominiums. *See* Fla. Stat. Ann. § 718.203 (West 1997). These warranties extend to both the developer and the contractor. The developer's implied warranty is a warranty of fitness or merchantability for the purposes or uses intended. The contractor's implied warranty is a warranty of fitness as to work performed or materials supplied. To comply with the statutory warranty of fitness, the contractor must provide work and materials that conform to the generally accepted standards of workmanship and performance of similar work and materials meeting the requirements specified in the contract. *Leisure Resorts, Inc. v. Frank J. Rooney, Inc.,* 654 So. 2d 911 (Fla. 1995). *See D.R. Horton, Inc. – Jacksonville v. Heron's Landing Condo. Ass'n of Jacksonville, Inc.,* 266 So. 3d 1201 (Fla. Dist. Ct. App. 2018, *reh'g denied* (2019)) (Although the defects did not force the homeowners to abandon their homes, the testimony certainly supported the jury's determination that the units did not meet the ordinary, normal standards that were reasonably to be expected of living quarters of comparable kind and quality).

The warranties established in Section 718.203 apply to defects that occur during the lifetime of the warranty (within three years of the date of completion of construction of the condominium or improvement). A condominium association has a statutory right to file suit on behalf of its unit owners for breach of implied warranty of fitness and merchantability for construction defects affecting the common interest. The time for filing suit does not begin until control of the association passes from the developer to the unit owners. *Toppino & Sons v. Seawatch at Marathon Condo. Ass'n,* 658 So. 2d 922 (Fla. 1994).

The parties can mutually agree to reallocate risks if the disclaimer is in clear and unambiguous language and clearly reflects both parties' expectations as to what items are not warranted. *Hesson,* 422 So. 2d at 946. Performance standards in a home warranty meet the requirements for disclaiming any implied warranty. *McGuire v. Ryland Group, Inc.,* 497 F. Supp. 2d 1356 (M.D. Fla. 2007) (Home Warranty does clearly reflect both parties' expectations as to which items are warranted and the extent to which the items are warranted and thus met the requirements for disclaiming any implied warranty). However, an express warranty does not automatically preclude an implied warranty. *McGuire v. Ryland Group, Inc.* 497 F. Supp. 2d 1347, 1351 (M.D. Fla. 2007).

Georgia

A licensed residential contractor and any affiliated entities shall offer a written warranty in connection with each contract to construct, or superintend or manage the construction of, any single-family residence where the total value of the work or activity or the compensation to be received by the contractor for such activity or work exceeds $2,500. The parties to the warranty may agree to submit any or all disputes arising under the warranty to arbitration. *See* O.G.C.A. §43-41-7.

A licensed residential contractor that enters into a covered contract shall provide a written warranty which describes, at a minimum:

(a) Covered work and activities;
(b) Covered exclusions;
(c) Standards for evaluating work and activities, which standards shall be those set forth in the current edition of the *Residential Construction Performance Guidelines* as published by the National Association of Home Builders;
(d) The term of the warranty, including commencement date(s) or event(s);
(e) Claim procedures;
(f) Contractor response options (such as repair, replace or compensate);
(g) Assignable manufacturer warranties.

See Georgia Administrative Code 553-7-01.

A builder expressly or impliedly promises that he or she has built the house in a fit and workmanlike manner. Implied in every contract by a builder-seller is the implied duty that the builder-seller performed the construction in a "fit and workmanlike manner." *Hall v. Harris,* 521 S.E.2d 638, 643 (Ga. Ct. App. 1999) (citing *Holmes v. Worthey,* 282 S.E.2d 919 (Ga. Ct. App. 1981), *aff'd* 287 S.E.2d 9 (Ga. 1982)). Thus, the law imposes upon the professional builder the obligation to exercise a reasonable degree of care, skill, and ability, the same degree of care and skill that others of the same profession would use under similar conditions and circumstances. *Schofield Interior Contractors, Inc. v. Standard Bldg. Co., Inc.,* 668 S.E.2d 316 (Ga. Ct. App. 2008); *Williams v. Runion,* 325 S.E.2d 441 (Ga. Ct. App. 1984). *See also Loyd H. Johnson Constr. Co., Inc. v. R & R Plumbing, Inc.,* 470 S.E.2d 283 (Ga. Ct. App. 1996) (regarding a leaking pipe). In *Hudgins v. Bacon,* 321 S.E.2d 359 (Ga. Ct. App. 1984), the court held that a builder has a contractual obligation to build the house in a fit and workmanlike manner.

A subsequent purchaser has no claim against a builder for breach of an implied warranty. *Moore v. Meek,* 483 S.E.2d 383 (Ga. Ct. App. 1997). An as-is clause in the sales contract can exclude any implied warranties. *Perrett v. Dollard,* 338 S.E.2d 56 (Ga. Ct. App. 1985).

Hawaii

Today, by common law or statutory law, an overwhelming majority of jurisdictions recognize an implied warranty in the purchase of new residential property. Forty-five states have adopted an implied warranty in some form and Hawaii appears to have done so in dicta. *Davencourt at Pilgrims Landing Homeowners Ass'n v. Davencourt at Pilgrims Landing, LC,* 221 P.3d 234 (Utah 2009) (citing *Ass'n of Apartment Owners of Newtown Meadows v. Venture 15, Inc.,* 167 P.3d 225, 246-248 (Hawaii 2007)).

Contractors engaging in home construction or home improvements shall, prior to obtaining a binding contract from the homeowner and prior to applying for a building permit[ ] . . . . [d]isclose all warranties, if any[.] Haw. Code R. § 16-77-79(a)(6). The implied warranty has no applicability to sales of undeveloped land or commercial premises. *Lindstrom v. Moffett Properties,* 2017 WL 1294001 (D. Haw. 2017).

Representations made to a prospective purchaser by a vendor concerning the condition of a dwelling are an express warranty. A warranty is an assurance by one party to a contract of the existence of a fact upon which the other party may rely. It amounts to a promise to indemnify the promisee for any loss if the fact warranted proves untrue. *Au v. Au,* 626 P.2d 173 (Haw. 1981).

Idaho

The vendor of a house under construction impliedly warrants that it will be completed in a workmanlike manner and would be reasonably fit for occupancy as a place to live. *Bethlahmy v. Bechtel,* 415 P.2d 698 (Idaho 1966) (builder failed to disclose the presence of an unsealed irrigation ditch through the lot and beneath the garage, and the basement was not of waterproof construction). *See Goodspeed v. Shippen,* 303 P.3d 225 (Idaho 2013) (This court has held that the implied warranty of habitability protects homebuyers against "major defects", which render the house unfit for habitation, and which are not readily remediable). *See also Ervin Constr. Co. v. Van Orden,* 874 P.2d 506 (Idaho 1994). Although an implied warranty of fitness does not impose upon a builder an obligation to deliver a perfect house, major defects that render the house unfit for habitation and that are not readily remediable entitle a purchaser to rescission and restitution. Defects susceptible of remedy ordinarily would not warrant rescission. The burden is upon the purchaser to establish facts that give rise to the implied warranty of fitness and its breach. *Bethlahmy,* 415 P.2d at 711.

Idaho extends the implied warranty to subsequent purchasers. *Tusch Enterprises v. Coffin,* 740 P.2d 1022, 1032 (Idaho 1987). The implied warranty of habitability extends to residential dwellings purchased for income-producing purposes that have never been occupied by purchasers. *Id.* Implied warranties may be disclaimed or waived, but the disclaimer must be clear and unambiguous, and courts will strictly construe it against the builder-vendor. *Tusch*, 740 P.2d at 1031; *Goodspeed*, 303 P.3d at 230 (One seeking the benefit of such a disclaimer must not only show a conspicuous provision which fully discloses the consequences of its inclusion but also that such was *in fact* the agreement reached. A knowing waiver of this protection will not be readily implied).

The implied warranty of habitability is not disclaimed where no mention is made of such warranty in the sales contract and the contract contains only general language stating that no warranties apply other than those contained within the four corners of the document. A party asserting waiver of the implied warranty of habitability bears the burden of proving that the other party knowingly waived it. *Tusch*, 704 P.2d at 1030–31.

An express three-year limitation for the quality of construction in a contract merely recited the duration of the warranty. It did not limit the time within which a lawsuit had to be filed. *See Conda Partnership, Inc. v. M.D. Constr. Co., Inc.*, 771 P.2d 920 (Idaho Ct. App. 1989).

Breach of the implied warranties of habitability and workmanship arise in contract. *See Petrus Family Trust Dated May 1, 1991 v. Kirk*, 415 P.3d 358 (Idaho 2018). In *Petrus* the Court dealt with Idaho Code § 5-241, which limits contract and tort actions stemming from the construction of an improvement on real property by providing that the applicable time period begins to run as of the date of the structure's completion. The Court determined that Idaho Code § 5-241 is a statute of repose because "its operation does not depend on the occurrence or discovery of injury." *Petrus*, 415 P.3d at 362. See also *Department of Environmental Quality v. Gibson*, 461 P.3d 706 (Idaho 2020). In *Petrus*, the claim brought by a subsequent purchaser was untimely, as it was required to have been brought within four years of completion of construction, since the contract for construction was oral. *Petrus*, 415 P.3d at 363.

Illinois

Implied in the contract for the sale of a new home by a builder-vendor is a warranty that the house—when completed and conveyed to the purchaser—will be reasonably suited for its intended use. The warranty, which also applies to developers, requires sellers to deliver homes that (a) are of at least fair average quality, (b) would pass without objection in the trade, and (c) are fit for the ordinary purpose of living in them. *Petersen v. Hubschman Constr. Co.*, 389 N.E.2d 1154 (Ill. 1979); *Tassan v. United Dev. Co.*, 410 N.E.2d 902 (Ill. Ct. App. 1980). The court held that an architect was not subject to the warranty of habitability in *Board of Managers of Park Point at Wheeling Condominium Ass'n v. Park Point at Wheeling, LLC.*, 48 N.E.3d 1250 (Ill. Ct. App. 2015) (finding that the warranty is traditionally applied to those who engage in construction). The warranty applies to builders of residential homes regardless of whether they are involved in the sale of the home. *1324 W. Pratt Condo. Ass'n v. Platt Constr. Group, Inc.*, 936 N.E.2d 1093 (Ill. Ct. App. 2010) (Pratt I) (Noting that since *Petersen,* the class of plaintiffs with standing to sue for violation of the implied warranty and the types of structures covered by the warranty has been expanded).

To establish a breach of warranty of habitability, a homeowner must prove that the home had a latent defect caused by an improper design, defective material, or poor workmanship that rendered the property unsuitable as a home. *Eickmeyer v. Blietz Org., Inc.,* 671 N.E.2d 795 (Ill. Ct. App. 1996). The warranty only applies to latent defects—defects that were not apparent to the purchasers when they viewed the property. *Park v. Sohn,* 433 N.E.2d 651 (Ill. 1982). In 2003, the Illinois Court of Appeals held that a buyer has a cause of action for breach of an implied warranty of habitability against a developer-seller for latent defects in improved land. *Overton v. Kingsbrooke Dev., Inc.,* 788 N.E.2d 1212, 1218 (Ill. App. Ct. 2003). The warranty extends to the sale of townhouses (*Colsant v. Goldschmidt,* 421 N.E.2d 1073 (Ill. Ct. App. 1981)) and condominiums (*Cooper v. United Dev. Co.,* 462 N.E.2d 629 (Ill. Ct. App. 1984)). However, as the implied warranty of habitability arises out of contract law, the purchaser of a newly constructed home may not pursue a claim for breach of an implied warranty of habitability against a subcontractor where there is no contractual relationship. *Sienna Court Condo. Ass'n v. Champion Aluminum Corp.,* 129 N.E. 3d 1112, 1129 (Ill. 2018). *See also 1400 Museum Park Condo. Ass'n by Board of Managers, v. Kenny Constr. Co.,* 200 N.E.2d 798 (Ill. Ct. App. 2021); (In this case there was no privity of contract between Kenny and the individual unit owners and therefore the Association could not pursue a claim for breach of implied warranty of habitability); *Goldfarb v. Bautista Concrete, Inc.,* 126 N.E. 3d 516, 520 (Ill. Ct. App. 2019); (A claim for breach of implied warranty of workmanship can only be brought if there is a direct contractual relationship between the homeowner and contractor/subcontractor).

It also extends to subsequent purchasers to the extent that they discover latent defects within a reasonable time after the original sale. *Redarowicz v. Ohlendorf,* 441 N.E.2d 324 (Ill. 1982). *See Sienna Court Condo. Ass'n v. Champion Aluminum Corp.,* 129 N.E. 3d 1112 (Ill. 2018) (Extending the implied warranty of habitability to subsequent purchasers of a home does nothing more than hold the builder-vendor to obligations arising from its original contract with the first purchaser and recognizes an implied assignment of the first purchaser's warranty rights with the second purchaser merely stepping into the shoes of the first purchaser). *But see, Fattah v. Bim,* 52 N.E.3d 332 (Ill. 2016) (The implied warranty of habitability may not be extended to a second purchaser of a house when a valid, bargained-for waiver of the warranty was executed between the builder-vendor and the first purchaser).

What constitutes a reasonable time, however, is unclear. In a recent case involving application of the implied warranty to a significant addition, the Illinois Supreme Court found that the 11-year period between the date of construction and the time the plaintiffs brought the action to be an unreasonable time to hold the contractor liable. *Von Holdt v. Barba & Barba Constr., Inc.,* 677 N.E.2d 836 (Ill. 1997). The measure of damages for breach of the implied warranty is the cost to repair the defects. However, if the defects can be corrected only at a cost unreasonably disproportionate to the benefit of the purchasers or if correcting them would involve unreasonable destruction of the work, the measure of damages is the amount by which the defects have diminished the value of the property. *Colsant,* 421 N.E.2d at 1077; *Park,* 433 N.E.2d at 464–65. The proper measure of damages for breach of implied warranty of habitability is the loss of value caused by defective brick. *Witty v. C. Casey Homes, Inc.,* 430 N.E.2d 191, 195–96 (Ill. Ct. App. 1981).

A builder may disclaim the implied warranty of habitability. *Petersen,* 389 N.E.2d at 1159. However, any disclaimer that does not reference the implied warranty of habitability by name is not a valid disclaimer of that warranty. *Bd. of Managers of Vill. Centre Condo. Ass'n, Inc. v. Wilmette Partners,* 760 N.E.2d 976, 981 (Ill. 2001). Consequently, because the disclaimer in this case did not refer to the implied warranty of habitability by name, that disclaimer was not effective to waive the warranty. *Id.* The disclaimer must be a conspicuous provision that fully discloses the consequences of its inclusion, and the vendor must show that the agreement between the parties in fact included the disclaimer. Accordingly, the court held that a disclaimer of "any and all implied warranties of merchantability and fitness as to the property" was part of the agreement between the parties and barred the action by the townhouse homeowner's association against the builder. The disclaimer was the only capitalized sentence in the entire contract. It was located near the space for signatures on the same page, and it indicated that in lieu of the implied warranties the purchaser would receive a particular warranty in a separate document. *County Squire Homeowners Ass'n v. Crest Hill Dev. Corp.,* 501 N.E.2d 794 (Ill. Ct. App. 1986). *See Board of Managers of Park Point at Wheeling*

Condo. Ass'n v. Park Point at Wheeling, LLC., 48 N.E.3d 1250 (Ill. Ct. App. 2015) (In Illinois, a disclaimer of a warranty of habitability is effective if it is a conspicuous part of the contract, refers to the warranty by name, and uses plain language that fully discloses the consequences of its inclusion); *1324 W. Pratt Condo. Ass'n v. Platt Constr. Group, Inc.*, 974 N.E.3d 279 (Ill. Ct. App. 2012).

The Illinois Court of Appeals, in *Bd. of Managers of Chestnut Hills Condo. Ass'n v. Pasquinelli, Inc.*, 822 N.E.2d 12, 19 (Ill. Ct. App. 2004), noted that the Illinois Supreme Court recognizes implied warranties of habitability as "a separate covenant between the builder vendor and the vendee because of the unusual dependent relationship of the vendee to the vendor." *Id.* (citing *Petersen v. Hubschman Constr. Co.*, 389 N.E.2d. 1154 (Ill. 1979)). The court in *Petersen* held that the burden required for waiver of that right is very high: "Although the implied warranty of habitability is a creature of public policy, we do not consider a knowing disclaimer of the implied warranty to be against the public policy of this State. However, we do hold that any such a disclaimer must be strictly construed against the builder-vendor." *Petersen,* 389 N.E.2d at 1159.

Furthermore, Illinois courts have ruled that the implied warranty of habitability does not extend to common areas where the defects do not interfere with the habitability of the owners' residences. In essence, the court held the warranty applicable where "latent defects" interfere with the owner's "reasonable expectation that the unit will be suitable for habitation." *Board of Dirs. of Bloomfield Club Rec. Ass'n v. The Hoffman Group, Inc.*, 712 N.E.2d 330, 334 (Ill. 1999) (citations omitted). The court further noted that "[w]hat is critical about this rule, therefore, is not simply that there be a hidden defect in or around a residence, but that the defect interfere with the dweller's use of that unit as a residence. This emphasis on a defect's interference with the habitability of one's residence is the key distinction between the implied warranty of habitability and other warranties." *Id.*

Indiana

Indiana statutory law provides that in the sale, or contract for sale, of a new home, the builder *may* warrant the following to the initial home buyer: (1) that the new home will be free from defects due to faulty workmanship for two years; (2) that the new home will be free from defects caused by faulty installation of plumbing, electrical, heating, cooling, or ventilating systems (excluding fixtures, appliances, or equipment items) for two years; (3) that the new home will be free from defects caused by faulty workmanship or defective materials in the roof or roof systems for four years; and (4) that the new home will be free from major structural defects for ten years. Ind. Code § 32-27-2-8 (a).

The warranties run to subsequent purchasers by the passing of legal or equitable title in the new home to a home buyer. Ind. Code § 32-27-2-8(b). The New Home Construction Warranty Act also allows a builder to disclaim all implied warranties if the text of the statute is followed. Ind. Code § 32-27-2-9. *Dinsmore v. Fleetwood Homes of Tennessee, Inc.,* 906 N.E.2d 186 (Ind. Ct. App. 2009).

In selling a model home, the builder may warrant to the home buyer that during the ten (10) year period beginning on the warranty date the model home will be free from major structural defects. Ind. Code § 32-27-2-8.5. The warranty survives the passing of legal or equitable title in the model home to a subsequent home buyer. The home buyer who purchases the model home from the builder shall, in writing on or before the date of closing or transfer of the model home to a subsequent home buyer, notify the subsequent home buyer of the warranty date and the amount of time remaining under the warranty.

Indiana also recognizes a common law implied warranty of fitness for habitation in connection with purchase of a new dwelling house from a builder-vendor. *Theis v. Heuer,* 280 N.E.2d 300 (Ind. 1987); *Corry v. Jahn,* 972 N.E.2d 907 (Ind. Ct. App. 2012); *Dinsmore,* 906 N.E.2d 186; *Russo v. Southern Developers, Inc.,* 868 N.E.2d 46 (Ind. Ct. App. 2007; Breach of the warranty is established by proof of a defect that substantially impairs the use and enjoyment of the residence as a place of human habitation. *R. N. Thompson & Assocs., Inc. v. Wickes Lumber Co.,* 687 N.E.2d 617 (Ind. Ct. App. 1997). The warranty of habitability applies to both site-built homes and manufactured homes. *Dinsmore,* 906 N.E.2d at 192. An amended complaint alleging that the windows and doors were installed improperly or were defective when supplied, a rafter was missing, there were exposed electrical wires, and there was water intrusion, were sufficient to put the builder on notice that the homeowners were suing for breach of the implied warranty of habitability. *ARC Const. Management, LLC v. Zelenak,* 962 N.E.2d 692 (Ind. Ct. App. 2012).

The warranty extends to a second or subsequent purchaser for latent or hidden defects that manifest themselves after the purchase and are not discoverable by the subsequent purchaser's reasonable inspection. Courts will apply a standard of reasonableness in light of surrounding circumstances. The age of a home, its maintenance, and the use to which the owner puts it are a few of the factors entering into this factual determination. *Barnes v. Mac Brown & Co., Inc.,* 342 N.E.2d 619 (Ind. 1976). In the case of a second or subsequent purchaser, the implied warranty of habitability protects the subsequent purchaser from latent defects not reasonably discoverable upon the purchaser's inspection and which manifest themselves after the purchase. *Smith v. Miller Builders, Inc.*, 741 N.E.2d 731, 740 (Ind. Ct. App. 2000) (citing *Barnes*, 342 N.E.2d at 621).

The court ruled that five years was not too long a period to extend the implied warranty of fitness for habitation as applied to a latent defect in a septic system. However, a homeowner cannot start a lawsuit against a builder-vendor for breach of implied warranty more than 10 years after substantial completion of the home. *Kissel*, 579 N.E.2d at 1327. A claim for breach of the implied warranty of habitability is subject to a six-year statute of limitations, with the claim accruing and the statute beginning to run "when the injured party knows or, in the exercise of ordinary, due diligence, could have known, that he or she sustained an injury." *Russo*, 868 N.E.2d at 48. The implied warranty of habitability applies only to home builders-vendors. *Choung v. Iemma*, 708 N.E.2d 7 (Ind. Ct. App. 1999). It does not apply to a mere vendor. *Id*.

The purchaser must at least inform the builder-vendor of the defect and give the builder-vendor a reasonable opportunity to cure or repair it. *Deckard v. Ratcliff*, 553 N.E.2d 523 (Ind. Ct. App. 1990). The measure of damages should be similar to the measure of damages recoverable under the implied warranty of merchantability, that is, the difference between the value as warranted less the value at the time of acceptance plus any incidental and consequential damages. *Jordan v. Talaga*, 532 N.E.2d 1174 (Ind. Ct. App. 1989).

Iowa

To establish breach of an implied warranty of workmanship in the sale of real estate, the owner must show five elements: (1) that the builder constructed the house to be occupied as a home; (2) the house was purchased from a builder-vendor, who constructed it for sale; (3) when sold, the house was not reasonably fit for its intended purpose or had not been constructed in a good and workmanlike manner; (4) at the time of purchase, the purchaser was unaware of the defect and had no reasonable means of discovering it; and (5) the purchaser suffered because of the defective condition. *Kirk v. Ridgway*, 373 N.W.2d 491, 496 (Iowa 1985).

The policy behind the implied warranty is to protect innocent homeowners who lack sophistication and bargaining power to protect themselves. *Rosauer Corp. v. Sapp Dev., LLC.*, 856 N.W.2d 906 (Iowa 2014). In *Rosauer*, after reviewing the public policy reasons underlying the implied warranty of habitability, the court declined to extend the implied warranty to the sale of land between developers able to protect themselves through express contract terms and simple soil tests, regardless of the work performed by the seller to make the lot buildable.

The theory of express warranty can apply to specific representations or warranties in contracts for the sale of real estate. For example, in *Flom v. Stahly*, 569 N.W.2d 135 (Iowa 1997), statements regarding construction of the exterior walls and ductwork for the heating system constituted express warranties. In *Reilly Const. Co., Inc. v. Bachelder, Inc.*, 2015 WL1331634 (Iowa Ct. App., March 25, 2015), the court affirmed that an express warranty may form the basis for recovery in a construction contract, even an oral construction contract. In *Reilly*, the court noted that the contractor who agreed to construct a pond, was expressly warranting that the pond would hold water. *Id.*

In defective-construction cases, the cost to repair the defect is the proper measure of damages. *Flom*, 569 N.W.2d at 142. The concept of economic waste limits the amount of the cost to repair. *Id.* Where the cost to repair is grossly disproportionate to the result, or to the benefit obtained, or if the repair involves the unreasonable destruction of the builder's work, then courts will find economic waste. *Id.* Damages may include diminution in value, cost of construction, completion in accordance with the contract, or loss of rentals. *Service Unlimited, Inc. v. Elder*, 542 N.W.2d 855 (Iowa Ct. App. 1995).

In a suit by subsequent purchasers against the builder of a custom home on a claim that defective construction caused water damage and mold, the Court of Appeals affirmed the district court ruling that the plaintiffs could not establish the elements of their implied warranty claim because they did not purchase the home from the builder/vendor. The court declined the plaintiffs' invitation to extend the protection of an implied warranty to a subsequent purchaser, holding that such a matter should be left to the state legislature. *Speight v. Walters Dev. Co., Ltd.*, 2007 WL 465572 (Iowa Ct. App. 2007). However, in 2008, the Iowa Supreme Court extended the implied warranty of habitability to a subsequent purchaser in *Speight v. Walter Dev. Co., Ltd.*, 744 N.W.2d 108 (Iowa 2008). In choosing to extend the implied warranty to subsequent purchasers, the court noted its purpose "is to ensure the home will be fit for habitation, a matter that depends upon the quality of the dwelling delivered not the [privity] status of the buyer." 744 N.W.2d at 113. *But see Luana Savings Bank v. Pro-Build Holdings, Inc.*, 856 N.W.2d 892 (Iowa 2014) (refusing to extend the implied warranty of workmanlike construction to protect a foreclosing lender that acquired a mold-infested apartment complex by deed in lieu of foreclosure).

Kansas

Kansas has recognized an implied warranty of fitness in the sale of new housing, at least when the seller built the house. *Scantlin v. Superior Homes, Inc.,* 627 P.2d 825 (Kan. 1981). The Kansas common law recognizes that, "when a person contracts to perform work or to render a service without express warranty, the law will imply an undertaking or contract on [that person's] part to do the job in a workmanlike manner and to exercise reasonable care in doing the work." *Scott v. Strickland,* 691 P.2d 45, 50 (Kan. Ct. App. 1984). The court held that in the absence of an express provision concerning workmanship, an implied warranty to perform in a workmanlike and reasonable manner exists with respect to building contracts. *Hennes Erecting Co. v. Nat'l Union Fire Ins. Co.,* 813 F.2d 1074 (10th Cir. 1987). In *Enfield v. Pitman Mfg.,* 923 F. Supp. 187 (D. Kan. 1996), the court ruled that under Kansas law, every contract for work or services includes an implied warranty that includes a duty to perform skillfully, carefully, diligently, and in a workmanlike manner. A homeowner may assert a tort or contract claim against a general contractor for substandard work depending on the nature of the duty allegedly breached. *David v. Hett,* 270 P.3d 1102 (Kan. 2011) (noting that contracts governing residential construction rarely involve the sophisticated parties with equal bargaining positions present in commercial products cases).

When does the statute of repose begin to run? According to one Kansas Court of Appeals decision the issuance of the certificate of occupancy does not trigger the period of repose. *Slatten v. R&S Builders, Inc.,* 2021 WL 5865562 (Kan. Ct. App., Dec. 10, 2021). In this case involving a claim by a subsequent purchaser against the builder, the court did not answer the question of when it begins to run, only that "To be clear here, we are not holding as a matter of law that the statute of repose starts when the owner of a new home occupies the dwelling or takes physical possession from the general contractor—only that the triggering act would not be later." *Id.* at *3. The court essentially agreed with the builder's position that "nothing of substance supports using a bureaucratic exercise— the issuance of the certificate of occupancy—that occurred well after it completed construction of the house and the Broadhursts took physical possession of the property." 2021 WL 5865562 at *3.

For purposes of the statute of limitations, "[t]he test to determine when an action accrues is that point when a plaintiff could have first filed and prosecuted an action to a successful conclusion." *Jeanes v. Bank of America,* 295 P.3d 1045 (Kan. 2013). K.S.A. 60–511(1) provides that "an action upon any agreement, contract or promise in writing shall be brought within five (5) years." In *Hewitt v. Kirk's Remodeling & Custom*

Homes, Inc., 310 P.3d 436 (Kan. Ct. App. 2013), which dealt with the question of when a cause of action for breach of the Repair or Replace Warranty accrues, the court held that pursuant to K.S.A. 60–511(1) a cause of action based upon a builder's express warranty to repair or replace construction defects in a newly built house must be brought within five years of the date the builder breached the warranty by refusing or failing to repair or replace the defects. The court made it clear that the warranty to repair is distinct from the warranty to deliver the house free of defects.

Kentucky

The sale of a new dwelling by a builder-vendor carries an implied warranty that, in its major structural features, the builder-vendor constructed the building in a workmanlike manner and with suitable materials. *Crawley v. Terhune,* 437 S.W.2d 743 (Ky. 1969) (concerning a suit that involved water in a basement). The implied warranty of habitability is an exception to the doctrine of *caveat emptor* (buyer beware) that otherwise applies to a purchase of a home. *Craig v. Keene,* 32 S.W.3d 90, 91 (Ky. Ct. App. 2000). *See also Ingram v. Oasis Investments, LLC.,* 2017 WL6508362 (W.D. Ky. Dec. 19, 2017) (Kentucky has recognized as a common law principle an implied warranty of habitability to the "buyer of a new house from the professional builder-seller[.]"). *See Miller v. Hutson,* 281 S.W.3d 791 (Ky. 2009) (declining to consider a further exception to the doctrine of *caveat emptor* extending the builder's exception to developers).

Privity (a relationship between the parties based upon a contract) is not necessary to collect damages for negligent construction. *Real Estate Mktg., Inc. v. Franz,* 885 S.W.2d 921 (Ky. 1994) (*overruled on other grounds by, Giddings & Lewis, Inc. v. Industrial Risk Insurers,* 348 S.W.3d 729 (Ky. 2011)).

Kentucky does not extend implied warranties to subsequent purchasers. *Real Estate Mktg.,* 885 S.W.2d at 926. *See Simpson v. Champion Petfoods USA, Inc.,* 397 F. Supp. 3d 952, 965 (E.D. Ky. 2019) (noting that the *Franz* court's holding, reaffirming the privity requirement, was unequivocal). A clause disclaiming an implied warranty must be conspicuous to draw the reader's attention to the clause. *Lagrew v. Hooks-SupeRx, Inc.,* 905 F. Supp 401 (E.D. Ky. 1995). *See Pippen v. Owensboro Master Builder, Inc.,* 2018 WL 4262791 (Ky. Ct. App., Sept. 7, 2018) (There is no legal authority in Kentucky that states that the warranty of habitability may not be expressly waived in this manner on a preprinted contract).

Moreover, Kentucky upholds the validity of contractual terms that deliberately depart from statutory limits by providing instead for shorter limitation periods. *Schultz v. Cooper,* 134 S.W.3d 618, 621 (Ky. Ct. App.

2003) (citing *Webb v. Kentucky Farm Bureau Ins. Co.*, 577 S.W.2d 17 (Ky. Ct. App. 1977)). Cited with approval in *Pippen*, 2018 WL 4262791 at *4. Thus, parties to a contract, such as in *Schultz* involving a contract for architectural services, may contract for a limitations period different from that provided by statute. 2018 WL 4262791 at *4. *See also* Ky. Rev. Stat. § 413.245. A "reasonable shortening of the statutory period of limitations does not ordinarily offend public policy." *Schultz,* 134 S.W.3d at 621. In *Schultz,* the court found that the parties agreed upon the contract terms and that they enjoyed equal bargaining power, and, consequently, "courts traditionally honor the ability of private parties on equal footing to structure their own affairs through contract. [Courts] are properly reluctant to interfere with clear contractual terms by re-writing them in the subsequent context of litigation." *Id.*

In addition, Kentucky has a "discovery rule," which is "a clearly worded default rule governing the date upon which a period of limitations begins." *Schultz,* 134 S.W.3d at 621 (citing Ky. Rev. Stat. § 413.245). The court in *Schultz* recognized that the parties deliberately selected a specific date for the accrual of any action and that the period deviated from the discovery rule in the statute. *Id.* The court reiterated that "such private deviations from the statute" are not unconscionable and do not violate public policy. *Id.* Rather, courts sanction "the validity of such provisions as part and parcel of the freedom of parties to fashion their own agreements." *Id.*

Louisiana

In 1986, the Louisiana Legislature enacted the New Home Warranty Act to promote commerce in Louisiana by providing clear, concise, and mandatory warranties for the purchasers and occupants of new homes. La. Rev. Stat. Ann. § 9:3141 *et seq.* Under the Act, a builder means any person, corporation, partnership, or other entity that constructs a home or any addition thereto, including a home occupied initially by its builder as his or her residence.

Subject to certain exclusions, the statute provides the following warranty periods: (1) for one year following the date the warranty commences, the home will be free from any defect resulting from noncompliance with the building standards; (2) for two years following the date the warranty coverage begins, the plumbing, electrical, heating, cooling, and ventilating systems will be free from any defect resulting from noncompliance with the building standards; and (3) for five years following the date the warranty commences, the home will be free from major structural defects resulting from noncompliance with the building standards. La. Rev.

Stat. Ann. § 9:3144. In addition, the provisions of this chapter may not be waived. La. Rev. Stat. Ann. § 9:3144(C); *Siragusa v. Bordelon,* 195 So. 3d 100, 106 (La. Ct. App. 2016). The act provides that any action to enforce warranties provided under the act is subject to a preemptive period of 30 days *after* the expiration of the appropriate time period in § 9:3144. *See* § 9:3146. Thus, for example, a one-year period is one year plus 30 days. *Ory v. A.V.I. Constr., Inc.,* 848 So. 2d 115 (La. Ct. App. 2003). A builder's warranty excludes any condition that does not result in physical damage to a residence. La. Rev. Stat. Ann. § 9:3144(B)(13); *Stokes v. Oster Dev., Inc.,* 807 So. 2d 987, 991 (La. Ct. App. 2002).

For a list of items excluded from the builder's warranty, see La. Rev. Stat. Ann. § 9:3144(B). The New Home Warranty Act also defines the terms "building standard" and "major structural defect." *See* La. Rev. Stat. Ann. § 9:3143. Warranty provisions apply when the builder-vendor violates applicable building codes or deviates from the plans and specifications for construction of the home. *Thorn v. Caskey,* 745 So. 2d 653, 660 (La. Ct. App. 1999). Furthermore, the building contract and attached specifications impose additional performance standards under the act and are enforceable under the act as part of a homeowner's breach of warranty action against a builder. *Graf v. Jim Walter Homes, Inc.,* 713 So. 2d 682 (La. Ct. App. 1998). Physical damage to the foundation systems and footings are "major structural defect[s]" within the meaning of that term in the Act. *Prestridge v. Elliott,* 847 So. 2d 789 (La. Ct. App. 2003). Courts have reaffirmed the requirement of physical damage as stated in the New Home Warranty Act. For example, in *Gines v. D.R. Horton, Inc.,* 2011 WL 3236097 (M.D. La. 2011), the court affirmed the unambiguous language of the statute which states that a builder does not warrant any "condition which does not result in actual physical damage to the home." *Id.* at *4. The *Gines* court distinguished its holding from *Graf* because Gines only alleged insufficient capacity of the air conditioning and heating system or improper installation of duct work but included no allegations that the home sustained any impending physical damage as a result. *Id.* at *4.

A warranty imposed under the Act transfers without charge to a subsequent purchaser. La. Rev. Stat. Ann. § 9:3148. Before bringing an action for breach of warranty, the owner must give the builder written notice within one year after knowledge of the defect, advising the builder of all defects and giving the builder a reasonable opportunity to comply with the Act's provisions. *Ory v. A.V.I. Constr., Inc.,* 848 So. 2d 115 (La. Ct. App. 2003) (finding plaintiffs filed suit 18 months after the date they discovered the defects); *Squyres v. Nationwide Housing Systems, Inc.,* 715 So. 2d 538 (La. Ct. App. 1998); *Graf v. Jim Walter Homes, Inc.,* 713

So. 2d 682 (La. Ct. App. 1998). The builder must give the owner written notice of the Act's requirements at the time of the closing. La. Rev. Stat. Ann. § 9:3145. Violation of the Act may subject the builder to an action for actual damages, including attorneys' fees. La. Rev. Stat. Ann. § 9:3149.

If the Act is applicable, it is the owner's exclusive remedy against the builder. *Melancon v. Sunshine Constr., Inc.,* 712 So. 2d 1011 (La. Ct. App. 1998); *see also Stokes v. Oster Dev., Inc.,* 807 So. 2d 987 (La. Ct. App. 2002). In *Stokes,* the court found that the exclusive remedy against a builder for water damage caused by alleged defects in the stucco material used for the exterior of the home was under the Act. *Id.* at 990. However, there may be circumstances present where the Act is not the sole remedy available to purchasers. For instance, a purchaser or owner could file suit for a breach of contract. In *Thorn v. Caskey,* 745 So. 2d 653, 655 (La. Ct. App. 1999), the owners sued the builder after the builder failed to complete the construction of the home pursuant to the terms of the contract. The appeals court found that the act was not the sole remedy available to the purchasers because they based their claims not only on the Act, but also on breach of contract principles. *Id.* at 663 (finding the record revealed the builder failed to do the work he contracted to do when he abandoned the home construction site and refused to return). *See also, Robinson v. Papania,* 207 So. 3d 566, 573 (La. Ct. App. 2016) (recognizing the NHWA is designed to protect the owner from faulty workmanship, but not to insure completion of the construction of a home under the terms of the contract). More recently, the Louisiana Supreme Court affirmed that principle when it found the New Home Warranty Act does not immunize a seller from other contract law provisions the seller is to follow in connection with the sale of the home. *Stutts v. Melton,* 130 So. 3d 808, 813 (La. 2013). In *Stutts,* the builder lived in the home for some time before selling it but failed to disclose the defective roof, and on appeal was held liable for fraudulent misrepresentations he made in the Residential Property Disclosure Statement.

By contrast, unlike the builder in *Thorn,* in *Siragusa v. Bordelon,* the builder defendant terminated the contract before completing the house, and as a result the house was completed through plaintiffs self-contracting, and subsequent occupancy of the house approximately eight months after defendant walked away. 195 So. 3d 100, 105 (La. Ct. App. 2016). But the court further noted that "[b]ecause none of the alleged damages were sustained by the [plaintiffs] in connection with securing completion of the construction . . . their damages were not related to any breach of contract. *Id.* (citing *Barnett v. Watkins,* 970 So. 2d 1028, 1036-1037 (La. Ct. App. 2007) (distinguishing *Thorn v. Caskey* by pointing out that when construction is completed by others and the homeowners accept the home by taking occupancy, there are no damages arising out of a breach of contract to build.)). The court held that "[c]onstruction defects and poor workmanship on the part of the builder are the types of defects squarely addressed by the NHWA. Thus, the trial court did not err in its determination that the NHWA provided the exclusive remedy in this case." *Siragusa,* 195 So. 3d at 105.

Louisiana's New Home Warranty Act does not apply to mobile homes. *Simmons v. Southern Energy Homes, Inc.,* 783 So. 2d 636 (La. Ct. App. 2001).

Imposition of warranties under the state New Home Warranty Act are aimed at the single builder of the entire structure and did not apply to a contractor who furnished work to only part of the home. Such a contractor is still subject to providing a workmanlike performance, free from defects in material and workmanship. This requirement is implicit in every building contract. *Allstate Enterprises, Inc. v. Brown,* 907 So. 2d 904 (La. App. 2 Cir. 2005).

Moreover, courts have found that a subcontractor cannot be a "builder" because it does not construct the entire structure "and deliver it to the owner as a new home." *See, Taylor v. Leger Constr., LLC,* 52 So. 2d. 1098 (La. Ct. App. 2010). *But see, Palermo v. Homes and More, Inc.,* 286 So. 3d 557, 563-64 (La. Ct. App. 2019) (distinguishing *Taylor* because defendant was hired as a general contractor of the construction at issue and even though defendant hired subcontractors to do all the work, it still met the definition of a "builder" under the NHWA since it was hired to construct the entirety of the house).

Maine

The implied warranty of habitability applies to the sale of a dwelling by a builder-vendor. *Banville v. Huckins,* 407 A.2d 294 (Me. 1979); *see also Stevens v. Bouchard,* 532 A.2d 1028 (Me. 1987) ("In Maine the law implies a warranty of habitability on the part of the builder-vendor in the sale of a new home."). *See also, Thompson v. Cloud,* 764 F.3d 82, 88 (1st Cir. 2014). The contractor warrants that the work will be performed in a reasonably skillful and workmanlike manner. An inadequate water system and a leak around the chimney may constitute a breach of warranty. *Wimmer v. Down East Properties, Inc.,* 406 A.2d 88 (Me. 1979).

Every minor defect in a new home does not necessarily make the structure uninhabitable. *Banville,* 407 A.2d at 297. In *Banville,* the court noted, "On the other hand, the warranty should not be defined in such strict terms as to require the defect to be of such magnitude as to require that the structure be deemed unlivable." *Id.* The warranty of workman-like performance does not expire after an arbitrary time period. *Parsons v. Beaulieu,* 429 A.2d 214 (Me. 1981). Ordinarily a contractor who completes a construction project in a workmanlike manner and in strict compliance with plans furnished by the owner will not be held liable for damages resulting from defects in the owner's specifications. *Paine v. Spottiswoode,* 612 A.2d 235 (Me. 1992). Generally, damages or defective performance under a construction contract may be measured either by the reasonable costs of reconstruction and completion in accordance with the contract or by the diminished value to the owner of the building caused by the defects. *Marchesseault v. Jackson,* 611 A.2d 95 (Me. 1992).

Maryland

In every sale, warranties are implied that at the time of delivery of the deed to a completed improvement or at the time of completion of an improvement not completed when the deed is delivered, the improvement is free from faulty materials, constructed according to sound engineering standards, constructed in a workmanlike manner, and fit for habitation. These warranties do not apply to any condition that an inspection of the premises would reveal to a reasonably diligent purchaser. Md. Code Ann., Real Prop. § 10 203; *see generally Morris v. Osmose Wood Preserving,* 667 A.2d 624 (Md. 1995). In addition, the statute specifically provides that these implied warranties cannot be excluded or modified by contract. *Savage v. Centex/Taylor, LLC,* 2012 WL 946698 (D. Md. 2012) (citing Md. Code Ann., Real Prop. § 203(d)). A new home means every newly constructed private dwelling unit in the state and the fixtures and structure that are made a part of a newly constructed private dwelling unit at the time of construction. *Andrulis v. Levin Constr. Corp.,* 628 A.2d 197 (Md. 1993); *see also, Lawley v. Northam,* 2011 WL 6013279 (D. Md. 2011) (reiterating that there is no implied warranty of habitability with respect to the sale of improved real estate in Maryland, except as to newly constructed homes).

Warranties do not expire on the subsequent sale of a dwelling by the original purchaser to a subsequent purchaser. The subsequent purchaser has continued protection until the warranties expire pursuant to § 10-204(b) (one year except for structural defects, which expires in two years). In determining whether an improvement is "fit for habitation," the test is one of reasonableness under the circumstances of the particular case. *Loch Hill Constr. Co. v. Fricke,* 399 A.2d 883 (Md. 1978). The following elements may create express warranties if made a part of the basis of the bargaining between the parties: (a) any written affirmation of fact or promise related to the improvement, (b) any written description of the improvement, including its plans and specifications, and (c) any sample or model. Md. Code Ann., Real Prop. § 10-202. Under Maryland law, when there is "[a]ny written affirmation of fact or promise which relates to [an improvement to real property] and is made a part of the basis of the bargain between the vendor and the purchaser," then "an express warranty that the improvement conforms to the affirmation or promise" is created. *Lemma v. CalAtlantic Group, Inc.,* 643 F. Supp. 3d 564 (D. Md. 2022) (citing Md. Code Ann., Real Prop. § 10–202(a)(1)).

Massachusetts

Generally, when a warranty accompanies a promise to repair or replace, that promise constitutes a specification of a particular remedy, rather than a negation of the warranty or the creation of an independent warranty. *New England Power Co. v. Riley Stoker Corp.,* 477 N.E.2d 1054, 1058 (Mass. App. Ct. 1985). Thus, "when there are a warranty and a promise to repair, the remedy of first resort is the promise to repair. If that promise is not fulfilled, then the cause of action is the underlying breach of warranty." *Id.*

If language that negates or limits a warranty is unreasonable, it must fail, and the court must give effect to the express warranty. *Id.* A modular home manufacturer breached an implied warranty that the modular home units sold to the plaintiffs would be fit for the ordinary purposes for which such goods are used because the roofs of those units were not watertight. *Burnham v. Mark IV Homes, Inc.,* 441 N.E.2d 1027 (Mass. 1982). When a party binds him or herself by contract to do work or to perform a service, that party agrees by implication to do a workmanlike job and to use reasonable and appropriate care and skill in doing it. *Wolov v. Michaud Bus Lines,* 484 N.E.2d 644 (Mass. 1985). A set of construction plans and specifications contain an implied warranty that they are accurate as to descriptions of the kind and quantity of work required. *Richardson Electrical Co., Inc. v. Peter Franchese & Son, Inc.,* 484 N.E.2d 108 (Mass. 1985).

The Massachusetts Supreme Court discussed the purposes behind implied warranties in *Albrecht v. Clifford,* 436 Mass. 706, 710 (Mass. 2002). There, the court stated that "[a]n implied warranty assures that consumers receive that for which they have bargained, an objectively habitable home." *Id.* (citations omitted). Furthermore, the court noted, "it protects purchasers from structural defects that are nearly impossible to ascertain by inspection after the home is built." *Id.* Moreover, an implied warranty "imposes the burden of repairing latent defects on the person who has the opportunity to notice, avoid, or correct them during the construction process." *Id. See, e.g., Berish v. Bornstein,* 878 N.E.2d 581, *4 (Mass. App. Ct. 2007) (unpublished opinion).

The court in *Albrecht* held that implied warranties are "independent and collateral to the covenant to convey and survive the passing of title to and taking possession of the real estate. [Implied warranties] cannot be waived or disclaimed, because to permit the disclaimer of a warranty protecting a purchaser from the consequences of latent defects would defeat the very purpose of the warranty." *Id.* at 47. The court further held that the implied warranty established in its opinion does not "apply to the purchase or sale of unfinished homes, where the parties may choose to waive or disclaim all warranties." *Id.* Nor did it make the builder-vendor an "insurer against any and all defects" in the home or impose an obligation "to deliver a perfect house, or to protect against mere defects in workmanship, minor or procedural violations of the applicable building codes, or defects that are trivial or aesthetic." *Id.*

In Massachusetts, to successfully establish breach of an implied warranty, a plaintiff must "demonstrate that (1) he purchased a new house from the defendant-builder-vendor; (2) the house contained a latent defect; (3) the defect manifested itself only after its purchase; (4) the defect was caused by the builder's improper design, material, or workmanship; and (5) the defect created a substantial question of safety or made the house unfit for human habitation." *Albrecht,* 767 N.E.2d at 47; *Berish v. Bornstein,* 770 N.E.2d 961, 971 (Mass. 2002). Furthermore, a plaintiff must bring the claim within the three-year statute of limitations and within the six-year statute of repose. *Albrecht,* 767 N.E.2d at 47 (citing Conn. Gen. Laws Ch. 260, § 2B (torts arising from improvements to real property)).

In *Berish,* the court considered "whether the implied warranty of habitability attaches to the sale of residential condominium units by a builder-vendor." *Berish,* 770 N.E.2d at 971. The court ruled, "an implied warranty of habitability attaches to the sale of new residential condominium units by builder-vendors in the Commonwealth, just as it now applies to the sale of new houses." *Id.* at 972. *See also, Trustees of Cambridge Point Condo. Trust v. Cambridge Point, LLC,* 88 N.E.3d 1142, 1151-1152 (Mass. 2018) (holding the rights of individuals to obtain legal redress when their homes fail to meet minimum standards, "whether grounded in the implied warranty of habitability or in the building code . . . are so vital that [the court has] consistently held that they cannot be waived.").

Michigan

An implied warranty of fitness is present in the sale of a new residential dwelling by a builder-vendor, whether the buyer purchases the home before, during, or after construction. In *Weeks v. Slavik Builder, Inc.,*

180 N.W.2d 503 (Mich. Ct. App. 1970), the dispute involved a leaky roof. The implied warranty of fitness and habitability run only to the initial purchaser of a new home. *McCann v. Brody-Built Constr. Co., Inc.,* 496 N.W.2d 349 (Mich. Ct. App. 1992).

An as-is clause waives the implied warranties that accompany the sale of a new home and imposes upon a purchaser the assumption of the risk of latent defects. *Lenawee County Bd. of Health v. Messerly,* 331 N.W.2d 203, 210 (Mich. Ct. App. 1982); *Coosard v. Tarrant,* 995 N.W.2d 87 (Mich. Ct. App. 2022) (an "'as is' clause in the parties' contract constitutes persuasive evidence that the purchaser assumed the risk of loss" however it does not transfer risk of loss where there is fraudulent misrepresentation before purchaser signs a binding agreement). A home purchaser could not recover damages for mental anguish arising from a builder's breach of implied warranty in the sale of a new home. *Groh v. Broadland Builders, Inc.,* 327 N.W.2d 443 (Mich. 1982).

A builder contracted to construct a custom home on an owner's land. Construction was substantially completed, and the owner occupied the custom home. Some jobs remained to be completed, including the finishing of hardwood floors. The subcontracted floor finisher left a bag of sawdust in the house that may have spontaneously combusted, causing a fire. The owner sued the builder for breach of the implied warranty of habitability. The court ruled that the builder was not liable under the implied warranty of habitability because it applied only to new homes sold as a part of a real estate transaction. The builder only entered into a construction contract with the owner and did not sell the land to him. *Smith v. Foerster-Bolser Constr., Inc.,* 711 N.W.2d 421 (Mich. Ct. App. 2006). *See also, Kisiel v. Holz, 725 N.W.2d 67* (Mich. Ct. App. 2006) (reaffirming *Smith* and holding that "[a] general contractor that agrees to construct a new home on land already owned by the purchaser is not a builder-vendor"); *Gold v. MG Building Co., Inc,.* 2023 WL 324151 (Mich. Ct. App. 2023) (holding the implied warranty of habitability applies only to the sale of new homes by a builder-vendor as part of a real estate transaction and does not extend to subsequent purchasers).

Minnesota

Minnesota allows recovery for a breach of implied warranty to purchasers who have a contractual relationship with a builder. *Robertson Lumber Co. v. Stephen Farmers Coop. Elevator Co.,* 143 N.W.2d 622 (Minn. 1966). Recovery may extend to include settling of the foundation where the foundation cracks and allows water to leak in. *Tereault v. Palmer,* 413 N.W.2d 283 (Minn. Ct. App. 1987). In *Buchman Plumbing*

Co., Inc. v. Regents of the University of Minn., 215 N.W.2d 479 (Minn. 1974), the court held that the third owner of a house could not recover from the builder because an implied warranty claim requires a direct contractual relationship between the parties. An express warranty can only arise by express provision of contract. *Id.* If a contract breach results in defective or unfinished construction and the loss in value to the injured party is not proven with sufficient certainty, the injured party may recover damages based on (a) the diminution in the market price of the property caused by the breach or (b) the reasonable cost of completing performance or of remedying the defects if that cost is not clearly disproportionate to the probable loss in value to him. *Rands v. Forest Lake Lumber Mart, Inc.*, 402 N.W.2d 565 (Minn. Ct. App. 1987).

In 1977, Minnesota enacted three statutory home warranties for purchasers of new residential construction. *Vlahos v. R&I Constr. Of Bloomington, Inc.*, 676 N.W.2d 672, 679 680 (Minn. 2004) (discussing the new home warranties) (citing Minn. Stat. §§ 327A.01-.07 (2002)). The warranties impose liability upon the builder for defects that occur during the applicable warranty period. *Id.* (citing Minn. Stat. § 327A.02, subd. 1). These statutory warranties begin to run from the time the initial vendee first occupies or takes title to the dwelling, whichever is earlier. Minn. Stat. § 327A.01, subd. 8 (2002). *See also, Village Lofts at St. Anthony Falls Ass'n. v. Housing Partners III-Lofts, LLC,* 937 N.W.2d 430 (Mich. 2020) (A breach of warranty claim under statute providing warranties to purchasers of new homes accrues when the homeowner discovers, or should have discovered, the builder's refusal or inability to ensure the home is free from major construction defects.). Although the warranties run with the dwelling and extend to subsequent purchasers, the warranty period does not begin anew when a subsequent purchaser occupies or takes title to the property. *Vlahos,* 676 N.W.2d at 679–80 (citing Minn. Stat. § 327A.01, subds. 6, 8).

Mississippi

Between a builder-vendor of a new home and the purchaser, an implied warranty provides that the builder-vendor built the home in a workmanlike manner and that it is suitable for habitation. Thus, in *Parker v. Thornton*, 596 So. 2d 854 (Miss. 1992), the failure to give notice of Yazoo clay was a failure to meet obligations in a workmanlike manner and a breach of implied warranties of fitness and habitability. *See also George B. Gilmore Co. v. Garrett*, 582 So. 2d 387 (Miss. 1991) ("Neither should plans and specifications which clearly do not take into account a construction problem of which the builder/contractor, the man with expertise should be well aware, remove from him all duty to warn. In such case the plans and specifications should not constitute an absolute defense."); *Caldarera v. Tennessee Log & Timber Homes, Inc.*, 2013 WL 5937396 (S.D. Miss. 2013). The implied warranty extends to subsequent purchasers. *Keyes v. Guy Bailey Homes*, 439 So. 2d 670 (Miss. 1983). The lack of privity is not a valid defense in a breach of implied warranties action of subsequent owners against the builder. *May v. Ralph L. Dickerson Constr. Corp.*, 560 So. 2d 729 (Miss. 1990).

Mississippi has a New Home Warranty Act that sets specific warranty periods for new homes. Miss. Code §§ 83-58-1 *et seq*. The act provides a one-year period that the home will be free from any defect due to non-compliance with the building standards. Miss. Code § 83-58-5(a). It also provides a six-year period that the home will be free from major structural defects due to noncompliance with the building standards. Miss. Code § 83-58-5(b). In *DiMa Homes, Inc. v. Stuart*, 873 So. 2d 140, 145 (Miss. Ct. App. 2004), the Mississippi Court of Appeals noted that this one-year period provides broad coverage. In addition, the act provides that six-years "following the warranty commencement date, the home will be free from major structural defects due to noncompliance with the building standards." *Id*. In *Townes v. Rusty Ellis Builder, Inc.*, 98 So. 3d 1046 (Miss. 2012), the state supreme court recognized that the claims under the New Home Warranty Act "do not 'accrue,' as the six-year warranty period is akin to a statute of repose[,] . . . which do so "regardless of the time of accrual of the cause of action or notice of the invasion of a legal right.'" 98 So. 3d at 1053. In *Townes,* the parties had entered into a tolling agreement, which the court found was unenforceable and therefore void because it did not set an end date. *Id*. at 1055.

The act defines building standards to mean "the standards contained in the building code, mechanical-plumbing code, and electrical code in effect in the county, municipality, or other local political subdivision where a home is to be located, at the time construction of that home is commenced, or, if the county, city, or other local political subdivision has not adopted such codes, the Standard Building Code, together with any additional performance standards, if any, which the builder may undertake to be in compliance." Miss. Code § 83 58-3(b). The "warranty commencement date" means "the date that legal title to a home is conveyed to its initial purchaser or the date the home is first occupied, whichever occurs first." *Id*. at § 83-58-3(g); *Townes v. Rusty Ellis Builder, Inc.* 98 So. 3d 1046, 1051 (Miss. 2012).

However, the Mississippi Court of Appeals held that "[r]egardless of the [New Home Warranty Act] or the contract, every building contract contains an implied term regarding reasonably skilled workmanship."

DiMa Homes, Inc. v. Stuart, 873 So. 2d 140, 145 (Miss. Ct. App. 2004). In *DiMa Homes*, the court noted that "[u]nless he represents that he has greater or less skill or knowledge, one who undertakes to render services in the practice of a profession or trade is required to exercise the skill and knowledge normally possessed by members of that profession or trade in good standing in similar communities." *Id.* (citing *George B. Gilmore Co.*, 582 So. 2d at 391–92 (quoting Restatement (Second) of Torts § 299A (1965)). Actions in negligence against a home builder have a three-year limitations period which begins to run from the date the owner takes possession of the house. *Smith v. DiMa Homes, Inc.*, 74 So. 3d 377, 378-79 (Miss. Ct. App. 2011).

Mississippi recognizes two methods for determining damages in construction contract suits. *DiMa Homes*, 873 So. 2d at 145. There, the court said, "Where a building is completed, substantially according to plans and specifications, the measure of damages may be determined by: (1) the cost rule, which is the cost of repairing the defects to make the building or structure conform to the specifications where such may be done at a reasonable expense if unreasonable economic waste is not involved, or (2) the diminished value rule, which is the difference in the value of the property with the defective work and what the value would have been if there had been strict compliance with the contract." *Id.* at 145. Furthermore, the court noted that the "'cost rule' allows recovery of the cost of repairing the defects to make the structure conform to specifications. However, such damages must not lead to economic waste. . . . The alternative measure is the difference in the value of the construction as built when compared to a properly completed project. That measure is used when awarding the cost to right what is wrong would be inequitable." *Id.* at 145–46.

In a dispute involving a road construction contract, the Mississippi Supreme Court held that a contractor should not be liable for performing the construction work according to the specifications provided by the owner. *Southland Enters. v. Newton County*, 838 So. 2d 286, 291 (Miss. 2003). In *Southland*, the court determined that although the county's specifications were insufficient, the contractor did not otherwise act negligently and was therefore not at fault. *Id.*

Missouri

Missouri recognizes an action for breach of an implied warranty of habitability by the purchaser of a new home against a builder-vendor regarding latent defects. The case involved the settling of concrete slabs upon which the house rested. *Smith v. Old Warson Dev. Co.*, 479 S.W.2d

795 (Mo. 1972); *see also Summer Chase Second Addition Subdivision Homeowners Ass'n v. Taylor-Morley, Inc.*, 146 S.W.3d 411, 415 (Mo. Ct. App. 2004) (noting this theory of recovery is a limited departure from the strict application of *caveat emptor*); *Hershewe v. Perkins*, 102 S.W.3d 73, 75 (Mo. Ct. App. 2003). *See also, Captiva Lake Investments, LLC v. Ameristructure, Inc.*, 436 S.W.3d 619, 629 (Mo. Ct. App. 2014). For the "*Old Warson* doctrine" to apply, it is imperative that the sale of the home be to the first purchaser of a newly constructed home, and that, "the builder and vendor are one and the same." *Hershewe*, 102 S.W.3d at 75 (quoting *Helterbrand v. Five Star Mobile Home Sales, Inc.*, 48 S.W.3d 649, 657 (Mo. Ct. App. 2001)); *Captiva Lake Investments, LLC*, 436 S.W.3d at 629. The "*Old Warson* doctrine" arose when the Missouri Supreme court first ruled that an implied warranty of quality and fitness applied to the purchase of residential real property. *Hershewe*, 102 S.W.3d at 75.

In *Hershewe*, "[t]he sole legal issue in contention is whether an exception to the *Old Warson* doctrine applies to the defective retaining walls. It is well established that the implied warranty of quality and fitness 'does not apply to an improvement outside the house, which is not an integral part of the structure or immediately supporting it.'" *Id.* (quoting *Wilkinson v. Dwiggins*, 80 S.W.3d 849, 851 (Mo. Ct. App. 2002)). Furthermore, the court noted, "it is logical that the doctrine of implied warranty and fitness in the sale of a new home does not apply to an item extraneous or unrelated to the home." *Hershewe*, 102 S.W.3d at 75 (citing *Old Warson*, 479 S.W.2d at 799 (buyer must "rely upon the fact that the vendor builder holds the structure out to the public as fit for use as a residence, and of being of reasonable quality")).

To recover for breach of implied warranty of habitability, the homeowner need not show negligence, knowledge, or fault on the part of the builder-vendor. *Allison v. Home Savings Ass'n of Kansas City*, 643 S.W.2d 847 (Mo. Ct. App. 1982); *Davies v. Barton Mut. Ins. Co.*, 549 S.W.3d 472 (Mo. Ct. App. 2017) (citing *Allison*, and further holding breach of implied warranty of habitability is not an "occurrence" under the insurance policy). Moreover, a contractor need not personally perform the actual construction to be held liable. *Id.* at 851. Breach of warranty may extend to damage from frozen pipes resulting from the improper installation of a water service line. *Stegan v. H. W. Freeman Constr. Co., Inc.*, 637 S.W.2d 794 (Mo. Ct. App. 1982).

The implied warranty of habitability targets structural defects that a builder-vendor has the opportunity to observe but fails to correct and that become latent through the construction process. *Hines v. Thornton*, 913 S.W.2d 373 (Mo. Ct. App. 1996); *see also, Captiva Lake Invs., LLC v. Ameristructure, Inc.*, 436 S.W.3d 619, 629 (Mo. Ct. App. 2014) (stating "[a] purchaser is granted a right of recovery against a builder-vendor under an implied warranty of habitability or quality where structural defects are present in consequence of poor workmanship or substandard materials or both."). However, in *Christensen v. R. D. Sell Constr. Co., Inc.*, 774 S.W.2d 535 (Mo. Ct. App. 1989), the implied warranty protected purchasers of a newly constructed home from latent nonstructural construction defects, including the driveway and front stairway, even though the purchasers continued to use them. *Trien v. Croasdale Constr. Co., Inc.*, 874 S.W.2d 478 (Mo. Ct. App. 1994). The implied warranty of habitability is reserved for the first purchasers of a new home from the builder-vendor. *Murray v. Crank*, 945 S.W.2d 28, 30 (Mo. Ct. App. 1997). The implied warranty of habitability also does not apply to multi-unit condominiums. *Captiva Lake Invs., LLC*, 436 S.W.3d at 629. When the purchaser seeks recovery from the builder for deterioration of the house purchased, the purchaser ought to give the builder notice of the deterioration and an opportunity to repair it. *Major v. Rozell*, 618 S.W.2d 293, 296 (Mo. Ct. App. 1981).

In Missouri, courts define workmanlike performance as "work which is completed in a skillful manner and is non-defective." *Waldroup v. Dravenstott*, 972 S.W.2d 364, 368 (Mo. Ct. App. 1998) (citing *Jake C. Byers, Inc. v. J.B.C. Investments*, 834 S.W.2d 806, 818 (Mo. Ct. App. 1992)); *see also, Mackey v. Schooler's Constr., LLC*, 640 S.W.3d 792, 798-99 (Mo. Ct. App. 2022).

Boilerplate clauses alone do not relinquish such warranties unless these occur through clear bargaining and negotiation. *Crawford v. Whittaker Constr., Inc.*, 772 S.W.2d 819 (Mo. Ct. App. 1989). *Boilerplate* is an industry term for standard language that is not original to that particular contract.

Montana

The builder-vendor of a new home impliedly warrants that the residence is constructed in a workmanlike manner and is suitable for habitation. The implied warranty of habitability of a dwelling house is limited to defects that are so substantial as to reasonably preclude the use of the dwelling as a residence. *Satterfield v. Medlin*, 59 P.3d 33, 36 (Mont. 2002) (overruled on other grounds by *Giambra v. Kelsey*, 162 P.3d 134 (Mont. 2007)); *Samuelson v. A.A. Quality Constr., Inc.*, 749 P.2d 73, 75 (Mont. 1988). The theory behind the implied warranty is not one of fault or wrongdoing; rather, it is based on the premise that the builder is in a better position to have prevented the problem. The implied warranty of habitability applies in an action in which an "amateur builder" (one who has built and sold at least two homes prior to the house in dispute) is a builder-vendor. *Pracht v. Rollins*, 779 P.2d 57 (Mont. 1989). The implied warranty of habitability by a builder vendor of a new home does not require that the home be built free of defects. *McJunkin v. Kaufman and Broad Home Sys., Inc.*, 748 P.2d 910 (Mont. 1987).

In Montana, residential construction contracts between a general contractor and an owner for the construction of a new residence must include certain disclosures and warranty requirements. Mont. Stat. Ann. § 28-2-2201. Where the construction consists of remediation or repair, the statutory requirements do not apply. In *Flathead Management Ptrs., LLC v. Jystad*, 454 P.3d 679 (Mont. 2019), the Montana Supreme Court held that because the plaintiff was a project manager rather than a general contractor, and the contract was not for the construction of a new home, the homeowner's contract with the plaintiff was not required to meet the state's statutory requirements for residential construction. 454 P.3d at 683. *See also,* Mont. Stat. Ann. § 28-2-2201. In this case, the court found that the contract was only to coordinate and facilitate remediation to a fire-damaged residence and property repair to guest quarters.

Nebraska

Implied warranties carry through to subsequent purchasers, but only in the case of "latent defects which manifest themselves after the subsequent purchase and are not discoverable by the subsequent purchaser's reasonably prudent inspection at the time of the subsequent purchase." *Moglia v. McNeil Co.*, 700 N.W.2d 608, 616–618 (Neb. 2005). Such liability is further subject to the statute of limitations found in the Nebraska statutes. *See* Neb. Rev. Stat. § 25-223.

A contractor constructing a building impliedly warrants that the building will be erected in a workmanlike manner and in accordance with good usage and accepted practices in the community where the work is done. *Henggeler v. Jindra*, 214 N.W.2d 925 (Neb. 1974); *see also Moglia,* 700 N.W.2d at 614; *Thurston v. Nelson,* 842 N.W.2d 631 644 (Neb. Ct. App. 2014). In *Henggeler*, the dispute involved a wet and damp basement. Where the damages are extensive, the owner may be entitled to rescind and/or void the contract, rather than accept money damages. In *Eliker v. Chief Industries, Inc.*, 498 N.W.2d 564 (Neb. 1993), the purchaser sought to rescind the contract because of the following: "a cracked driveway, the drain tile allowed water to drain into the garage, numerous foundation cracks, severe cracks in basement walls, an exterior wall that was bowed inward 1 to 2 inches, water seepage in the basement and the garage, and doors out of alignment." The court in *Eliker* found that "the purchaser of a new home expects it to be, at the very least, structurally sound and habitable [ ] and should not be faced with the virtual impossibility of resale because of the home's latent defects." 498 N.W.2d at 570 (holding that recission was the proper remedy where breach of contract is so fundamental as to defeat the object of the parties in making the agreement). A construction contract specifying that all work and materials were guaranteed for one year was not exclusive and did not bar recovery for defective work discovered more than one year after the date of substantial completion. *The Omaha Home for Boys v. Stitt Constr. Co., Inc.*, 238 N.W.2d 470 (Neb. 1976).

In *Adams v. Manchester Park, LLC*, 871 N.W.2d 215 (Neb. 2015), the Nebraska Supreme Court found that the existence of a 1-year express warranty, which was issued after substantial completion of the home, does not extend the statute of limitations for the homeowners' claims. In *Adams,* plaintiffs alleged a breach of the implied duty to perform in a workmanlike manner, a breach of the implied warranty of habitability, negligent construction, fraudulent concealment of material facts, and breach of the 1-year express warranty. *Id.* at 219. However, the plaintiffs did not claim that defendant "failed to make repairs when requested to do so pursuant to the express warranty" and accordingly the court held the one-year express warranty did not extend Nebraska's statute of limitations on the homeowners' claims. *Id.* at 220.

An express common law warranty arises when, to induce a sale, the seller makes a statement of fact representing the quality or character of the thing sold, and the buyer reasonably relied upon that statement. *Herman v. Bonanza Buildings, Inc.*, 390 N.W.2d 536 (Neb. 1986).

In *Moglia*, subsequent purchasers filed suit against the original general contractor and its trade contractors for construction defects, citing a breach of an implied warranty of workmanlike performance and a breach of an implied warranty of habitability. The Nebraska Supreme Court ruled as follows:

- Subcontractors are not subject to the implied warranty of workmanlike performance because they have no direct contractual relationship (privity) with the owner.
- Because general contractors are in privity with owners, they are subject to the implied warranty of workmanlike performance. In the opinion of the Court, builders should not be relieved of this liability simply because the property changed hands. Therefore, the Court extended the implied warranty of workmanlike performance to subsequent purchasers.

■ Despite an awareness that an implied warranty of habitability has been adopted in many states, the Court ruled that Nebraska has not adopted this cause of action, and therefore, it does not extend an implied warranty of habitability to either original or subsequent purchasers.

Moglia v. McNeil Company, Inc., 700 N.W.2d 608 (Neb. 2005).

Nevada

The implied warranty of habitability reflects natural and sound public policy, and a builder-vendor of a house is subject to this implied warranty, as well as the contractor who constructed the house. For example, in *Radaker v. Scott*, the court found the builder-vendor and the contractor liable for a breach of the implied warranty of habitability because they were joint venturers. *Radaker v. Scott*, 855 P.2d 1037 (Nev. 1993). Courts have held that "[i]n order to claim breach of the implied warranty of habitability, a plaintiff must demonstrate that he or she purchased a new dwelling from the defendant." *Sedona Condo. Homeowners Ass'n, Inc. v. Camden Dev., Inc.*, 381 P.3d 661 (Nev. 2012) (citing *Radaker*, 855 P.2d at 1039). The Sedona court found that plaintiff's members did not purchase certain units from either of the defendants, and therefore no contract existed between plaintiffs and defendants, and no vertical privity existed. *Id.* Further, defendants were not builder-vendors of a new dwelling and the units started out as apartments, not condominiums and therefore the implied warranty of habitability did not apply. *See also, Bour Enterprises, LLC v. 4520 Arville*, 516 P.3d 1112, *1 (Nev. 2022) (unpublished opinion) (declining to extend the implied warranty of habitability to the duties owed by commercial landlords).

In *Calloway v. City of Reno*, the court noted that a family can already assert express and implied warranties to recover damages from a builder-vendor for defects in new construction. 939 P.2d 1020 (Nev. 1997) (reh'g granted and withdrawn by *Calloway v. City of Reno*, 971 P.2d 1250 (Nev. 1998). In 2000 again on rehearing, the Nevada Supreme Court adopted the principle that the economic loss doctrine applies to construction defect cases. *Calloway v. City of Reno*, 993 P.2d 1259 (Nev. 2000) (*Calloway II*). However, the Nevada Supreme Court limited *Calloway II* by recognizing claims for negligence may be stated directly under Nevada Statute § 40.600 *et seq.* dealing with construction defects. *Olson v. Richard*, 89 P.3d 31, 33 (2004) (citing Nev. Rev. Stat. § 40.640 for the proposition that "a contractor is liable for any construction effects resulting from his acts or omissions or the acts or omissions of his agents, employees, or subcontractors").

New Hampshire

New Hampshire recognizes the existence of an implied warranty of habitability and workmanlike quality in the sale of a house as an obligation imposed on a builder or contractor. *Healy v. Telge*, 653 A.2d 1118 (N.H. 1995); *Norton v. Burleaud*, 342 A.2d 629 (N.H. 1975) (recognizing that in a claim for breach of implied warranty to construct a residential home that the home be constructed in a workmanlike manner and in accordance with accepted standards). *See also, Sheridan v. Page,* 2018 WL 4375107 (D. N.H. 2018) (citing *Norton v. Burleaud* and concluding plaintiffs' allegations were sufficient to state claims for breach of contract and breach of implied warranties). The warranty extends to subsequent purchasers of property in the case of latent defects that become manifest after the subsequent owner's purchase and that were not discoverable upon a reasonable inspection of the structure prior to the purchase. *Lempke v. Dagenais*, 547 A.2d 290 (N.H. 1988); *see also Page v. Willey*, 648 A.2d 206 (N.H. 1994).

New Jersey

New Jersey recognizes both statutory and common law warranties. The statutory warranty, New Home Warranty and Builders' Registration Act, N.J. Stat. Ann. § 46:3B-2, is supplementary to, and not exclusive of, those provided by common law. *See The Terrace Condo. Ass'n v. Midatlantic Nat'l Bank*, 633 A.2d 1060 (N.J. Super. Ct. Law Div. 1993). *Terrace* involved leakage into units, terraces, and parking decks, and dampness on outside walls. *Id.* at 1065. The statutory warranty provides for one-year (workmanship), two-year (systems), and 10-year coverage (major construction defects). *Id. See also Ingraham v. Trowbridge Builders*, 687 A.2d 785, 789–90 (N.J. Super. App. Div. 1997) (finding the warranty date began with occupancy by the owner, not the builder's use of the home as a model). The common law warranty arises whenever a consumer purchases from someone who holds himself out as a builder-vendor of new homes. *McDonald v. Mianecki*, 398 A.2d 1283 (N.J. 1979) (involving a dispute over the potability of the water supply to the house).

New Jersey courts make clear that, "as a matter of justice and fair dealing, the buyers of new homes are entitled to the benefit of an implied and far-reaching warranty of habitability." *Nobrega v. Edison Glen Assocs.*, 772 A.2d 368 (N.J. 2000) (citing McDonald v. Mianecki, 398 A.2d 1283 (1979); *Schipper v. Levitt & Sons, Inc.*, 207 A.2d 314 (N.J. 1965)). The New Jersey Supreme Court has also construed the New Home Warranty Act in conjunction with the [Contractors' Registration Act], to provide "a seamless web of protections for the homeowner." *Remote Risk Management, LLC v. LoGrasso Builders*, 2019 WL 1111105 (N.J. Super. Ct. App. Div. 2019) (citing *Czar, Inc. v. Heath*, 966 A.2d 1008 (N.J. 2009).

In *Czar, Inc.*, the New Jersey Supreme Court held the Contractors' Registration Act (CRA) applied to the agreement between the contractor and the homeowner for a kitchen remodel because the house was newly built, but not yet permitted or occupied. 966 A.2d at 1016. The court found that "[t]hese two statutes represent a carefully created series of obligations imposed on contractors, each providing the homeowner with certain protections. There is no place in them for a contractor to use the one with which it did not comply as a sword against the homeowner whose rights the Legislature intended to protect." *Id.*

The implied warranty encompasses reasonable workmanship and habitability, and breach of the implied warranty of reasonable workmanship may also constitute a breach of the implied warranty of habitability if the condition is sufficiently serious to affect the dwelling's habitability. *Aronsohn v. Mandara*, 484 A.2d 675 (N.J. 1984). Both statutory and common law warranties extend to subsequent purchasers. New Jersey Stat. Ann. § 46:3B-4. The New Home Warranty and Builders' Registration Act "imposes responsibility upon a new home builder for any covered defect occurring during an applicable warranty period [ ] which includes a ten-year period for major construction defects[.]" *Lakhani v. Bureau of Homeowner's Prot., New Home Warranty, Dept. of Cmty. Affairs*, 811 A.2d 918 (N.J. Super. Ct. App. Div. 2002) (citing New Jersey Stat. Ann. § 46:3B-4).

New Mexico

A warranty is an assurance by one party to a contract of the existence of a fact upon which the other party may rely. A warranty may be either express or implied, and once a court determines a warranty exists, the seller's liability remains the same whether the breach pertains to an express or implied warranty. *Camino Real Mobile Home Park P'ship v. Wolfe*, 891 P.2d 1190 (N.M. 1995) (*overruled on other grounds by Sunnyland Farms, Inc. v. Central New Mexico Elec. Co-op., Inc.*, 301 P.3d 387 (N.M. 2013) (holding the proper test for consequential damages in New Mexico is the standard as interpreted in Restatement (Second) of Contracts § 351).

In a home constructed by a builder that had no duct or subterranean water drainage problems, the express terms of the written contract between the builder and the purchasers negated the existence of any implied warranties of habitability. *Newcum v. Lawson*, 684 P.2d 534 (N.M. Ct. App. 1984). However, "a warranty that a building will be erected in a workmanlike manner, free from any material defects, constitutes a contractual agreement that the work will be performed in a proper manner, and that there do not exist any significant defects in the structure." *Id.* at 540. *See also, Smith v. Moore,* 2018 WL 6583367, *1 (N.M. Ct. App. 2018) (finding plaintiff failed to explain why she was entitled to a greater right than currently recognized in New Mexico (relying on *Newcum v. Lawson*)).

In addition, New Mexico has not adopted an implied warranty of habitability in the purchase of new residential property. *Cowan v. D'Angelico,* 2010 WL 9067968, *3 (D. N.M. 2010) (noting that while most states recognize implied warranties of habitability in new homes, New Mexico does not). New Mexico has also rejected the implied warranty in landlord-tenant situations. *Smith v. Moore,* 2018 WL 6583367, *1 (N.M. Ct. App. 2018).

New York

New York statutory law provides that the contract, or agreement for the sale of a new home, include a housing merchant implied warranty. A housing merchant implied warranty provides that:

a. One year from and after the warranty date the home will be free from defects due to a failure to have been constructed in a skillful manner.
b. Two years from and after the warranty date the plumbing, electrical, heating, cooling, and ventilation systems of the home will be free from defects due to a failure by the builder to have installed such systems in a skillful manner; and
c. Six years from and after the warranty date the home will be free from material defects.

N.Y. Gen. Bus. § 777-a(1)(a)-(c). The Housing Merchant Implied Warranty may be excluded or modified by the builder or seller of a new home only if the buyer is offered a limited warranty in accordance with the following provisions:

a. A copy of the express terms of the limited warranty shall be provided in writing to the buyer for examination prior to the time of the buyer's execution of the contract or agreement to purchase the home.
b. A copy of the express terms of the limited warranty shall be included in, or annexed to and incorporated in, the contract or agreement.
c. The language of the contract or agreement for sale of the home must conspicuously mention the housing merchant implied warranty and

provide that the limited warranty excludes or modifies the implied warranty. Language to exclude all implied warranties is sufficient if it states, for example, that "There are no warranties which extend beyond the face hereof."

d. The limited warranty shall meet or exceed the standards provided in subdivisions four and five of this section.

N.Y. Gen. Bus. § 777-b(3)(a)-(d).

In addition, N.Y. Gen. Bus. § 777-b (4) states "[a] limited warranty sufficient to exclude or modify a housing merchant implied warranty must be written in plain English and must clearly disclose: (a) that the warranty is a limited warranty which limits implied warranties on the sale of the home; the words 'limited warranty' must be clearly and conspicuously captioned at the beginning of the warranty document; (b) the identification of the names and addresses of all warrantors; (c) the identification of the party or parties to whom the warranty is extended and whether it is extended to subsequent owners . . . . (g) the term of the warranty coverage and when the term begins[ ]; [and] (h) step-by-step claims procedures required to be undertaken by the owner, if any, including directions for notification of the builder and any other warrantor. . . ." *Odze v. Orange County Builders, LLC,* 170 N.Y.S.3d 846, 852 (N.Y. Cit. Ct. 2022). In *Odze,* the court found that the defendant attempted to limit the warranty to before closing of title, and therefore did not satisfy the requirements of section 777-b. Instead, the statutory housing merchant implied warranty in section 777-a applied and required the defendant to correct the defective steps to the home. 170 N.Y.S.3d at 852-853.

A builder-vendor impliedly warrants that he or she constructed a house in a skillful manner, free of material, latent defects. *Merritt v. Hooshang Constr., Inc.,* 628 N.Y.S.2d 792, 794 (N.Y. 1995) (citing N.Y. Gen. Bus. § 777-a). *See also, Lupien v. Bartolomeo,* 799 N.Y.S.2d 161, *6 (N.Y. Sup. Ct. 2004) (stating "Courts are not fond of disclaimers and do not hesitate to apply warranties of skillful work free from material latent defects.") (internal citations omitted).

The implied warranty statute only applies to contracts or agreements that involve the sale of new homes. *Watt v. Irish,* 708 N.Y.S.2d 264 (N.Y. 2000); *116 Waverly Place LLC v. Spruce 116 Waverly LLC,* 119 N.Y.S.3d 78, 79 (N.Y. Sup. Ct. App. Div. 2020) (confirming that "the gut-renovated townhouse was not a 'new home' under [N.Y. Gen. Bus. Law] 777(5)."). In *Garan v. Don & Walt Sutton Builders, Inc.,* the court held the statutory provisions of § 777-a did not govern the case because it involved a "custom home" as defined by N.Y. Gen. Bus. § 770(7). *Garan v. Don & Walt Sutton Builders, Inc.,* 773 N.Y.S.2d 416 (N.Y. 2004). Therefore, the contract is one for "home improvement" (§ 770(3)) and is governed by General Business Law article 36-A. *Id. See also Biggs v. O'Neill,* 766 N.Y.S.2d 391, 392 (N.Y. 2003). Pursuant to § 772(2), "[n]othing in [article 36-A] shall impair, limit, or reduce the statutory, common law or contractual duties or liability of any contractor." *Id.* at 416. Accordingly, "the notice condition precedent provisions of General Business Law article 36-B (General Business Law § 777 a (4)) have no application to this case." *Id.* at 417.

In *Biggs,* the court held that the housing merchant warranty "has no application to a contract for the construction of a 'custom home'" on non-builder-owned property, which is afforded protection under General Business Law article 36-A. *Biggs,* 766 N.Y.S.2d at 392. However, a lower-level New York court took the opposite position when it found that the new home implied warranties act also applied to custom homes. *See Gorsky v. Triou's Custom Homes,* 755 N.Y.S.2d 197 (N.Y. Sup. Ct. 2002) (holding that statutory new home implied warranties apply to custom homes). Builders should exercise caution when analyzing whether the act will apply to custom homes.

Courts have also found that the statutory housing merchant warranty does not apply to condominiums in buildings that have more than five stories. *Tribeca Space Managers, Inc. v. Tribeca Mews Ltd.,* 117 N.Y.S.3d 808, *4. In *Tribeca Space Managers,* the court stated, the statute "defines 'new home' to include a 'for-sale unit in a multi-unit residential structure' under a condominium regime only where that structure is 'five stories or less.'" *Id.* at *4 (citing N.Y. Gen. Bus. § 777(5)). In this case, the court noted that the "'housing merchant implied warranty' itself exists only in a 'contract or agreement for sale of a new home.' It thus does not apply to contracts for the sale of condominium apartments in a building of more than five stories. The building in this case is ten stories tall." *Id.*

Where a plaintiff homeowner does not comply with the notice provisions set out in the new home warranty statute, courts will dismiss the claims. *See, e.g., Taggart v. Martano,* 723 N.Y.S.2d 211, 212 (N.Y. Sup. Ct. 2001); *Rushford v. Facteau,* 669 N.Y.S.2d 681, 681 (N.Y. Sup. Ct. 1998) (holding that the purchasers failed to give builders notice of claim, which alleged failure to construct the house in a skillful manner, within 30 days after expiration of one-year warranty period, as required by statute as condition precedent to bringing a claim) (citing N.Y. Gen. Bus. § 777-a(1)(a)); *Rosen v. Watermill Dev. Corp.,* 768 N.Y.S.2d 474, 475 (N.Y. Sup. Ct. 2003).

The builder may exclude or modify all express and implied warranties, including the housing merchant implied warranty created by the statute or by common law provided that the purchase agreement contains a limited warranty in accordance with the provisions of the General Business

Law § 777-b. A claim based on a breach of implied warranty between a builder-vendor and purchaser of a house can only arise at closing of title. If no closing and no sale of the house occurs, the purchaser's claim for breach of implied warranty is not viable. *See Pitcherello v. Moray Homes, Ltd.*, 540 N.Y.S.2d 387 (N.Y. Sup. Ct. 1989).

North Carolina

In North Carolina, in every contract for the sale of a recently completed dwelling and in every contract for the sale of a dwelling under construction, the vendor in the business of building such dwellings shall be held to impliedly warrant to the initial purchaser that, at the time of the passing of the deed or the taking of possession by the purchaser, the dwelling, together with all its fixtures, is sufficiently free from major structural defects, and it is constructed in a workmanlike manner to meet the standard of workmanlike quality then prevailing at the time and place of construction. *Gaito v. Auman*, 327 S.E.2d 870 (N.C. 1985); *Hartley v. Ballou*, 209 S.E.2d 776 (N.C. 1974); *Lincoln v. Bueche*, 601 S.E.2d 237 (N.C. Ct. App. 2004); *Becker v. Graber Builders, Inc.*, 561 S.E.2d 905 (N.C. Ct. App. 2002).

Implied warranties do not apply to the sale of used residences by their owners. *Everts v. Parkinson*, 555 S.E.2d 667 (N.C. Ct. App. 2001). Implied warranty law that is applicable to single-family homes is also applicable to condominiums. N.C. Gen. Stat. § 47C-4-114 (2005). In *Lumsden v. Lawing*, 421 S.E.2d 594 (N.C. Ct. App. 1992), the purchasers were entitled to void the contract for acquisition of the home because of the builder's breach of warranty of fitness for use as a single-family home. The purchasers were also entitled to sums expended by them on mortgage interest and insurance premiums. In *Lapierre v. Samco Dev. Corp.*, 406 S.E.2d 646 (N.C. Ct. App. 1991), the dispute involved the construction of a garage and a driveway. In *George v. Veach*, 313 S.E.2d 920 (N.C. Ct. App. 1984), the court found the builder liable for breach of implied warranty for a defective septic system, notwithstanding that the county health department oversaw the builder's construction and approved the completed system. *See also Lyon v. Ward*, 221 S.E.2d 727 (N.C. Ct. App. 1976). In *Kenney, v. Medlin Constr. & Realty Co.*, 315 S.E.2d 311 (N.C. Ct. App. 1984), the court held that the cost of repair, rather than the diminution in value, was the proper measure of damages, unless repair would require that a substantial part of the completed work be destroyed.

In *Ford v. All-Dry of the Carolinas, Inc.*, 711 S.E.2d 876, *8 (N.C. Ct. App. 2011), the court recognized that "[w]hen a party contracts to install something, there exists an implied warranty that it will be installed in a workmanlike manner." 711 S.E.2d at *8 (citing *Cantrell v. Woodhillm Enters.,*

160 S.E.2d 476, 481 (N.C. 1968) ("It is the duty of every contractor or builder to perform his work in a proper and workmanlike manner, and he impliedly represents that he possesses the skill necessary to do the job he has undertaken.")).

A builder-vendor and a purchaser can enter into a binding agreement that the implied warranty of habitability would not apply to their particular transaction. However, such exclusion, if desired by the parties to a contract for the purchase of a residence, should be accomplished by clear, unambiguous language, reflecting the fact that the parties fully intended to achieve such a result. *Bass v. Pinnacle Custom Homes*, 592 S.E.2d 606 (N.C. Ct. App. 2004); *Allen v. Roberts Constr. Co.*, 532 S.E.2d 534, 543 (N.C. Ct. App. 2000). The warranty arises by operation of law and imposes strict liability on the builder-vendor. *Medlin v. FYCO, Inc.*, 534 S.E.2d 622, 627 (N.C. Ct. App. 2004) (noting in this case "there was substantial evidence that plaintiffs' house failed in the essential requirement of keeping moisture out, a major structural defect").

North Dakota

An implied warranty of fitness may be applied to the construction of a residential home. *Barnes v. Mitzel Builders, Inc.*, 526 N.W.2d 244, 246 (N.D. 1995). In *Carlson Homes, Inc. v. Messmer*, 307 N.W.2d 564 (N.D. 1981), a claim of landscaping done in an unworkmanlike manner outlined the warranty theory. In *Dobler v. Malloy*, 214 N.W.2d 510 (N.D. 1973), the case involved a claim of a defective joist system.

North Dakota law "recognizes an implied warranty of fitness for the purpose in construction contracts." *Bakke v. Magi-Touch Carpet One Floor & Home, Inc.*, 920 N.W.2d 726 (N.D. 2018); *Leno v. K & L Homes, Inc.* 803 N.W.2d 543 (N.D. 2011); *Dobler v. Malloy*, 214 N.W.2d 510 (N.D. 1973). Further, the court recognizes that the existence of an implied warranty of fitness for a particular purpose in a construction contract, and the breach of that warranty, are findings of fact." *Bakke*, 920 N.W.2d at 730 (citing *Air Heaters, Inc. v. Johnson Elec., Inc.*, 258 N.W.2d 649, 654 (N.D. 1977)). Further, the North Dakota Supreme Court has held that all warranties may properly be excluded, but that exclusion must be part of the bargain between the parties. *See Leno v. K&L Homes, Inc.*, 803 N.W.2d 543 (N.D. 2011).

Ohio

In Ohio, a builder-vendor has a duty to construct in a workmanlike manner using ordinary care. *Velotta v. Leo Petronzio Landscaping, Inc.*, 433 N.E.2d 147 (Ohio 1982). This is a duty required by law and it cannot be waived by the homeowner. *Jones v. Centex Homes*, 967 N.E.2d 1199 (Ohio 2012).

Breach of the warranty to construct in a workmanlike manner is a negligence action even though it may arise out of contract. *Dillon v. Ferris*, 1996 WL 323685 (Ohio Ct. App. 1996) (unpublished opinion). However, in *Faber v. Ronald Chaffman General Constr., Inc.*, the court found that if a plaintiff brings an action sounding in tort and bases his claim upon a theory or duty owed by a defendant as a result of contractual relations, he must be a party or privy to the contract in order to prevail. 930 N.E.2d 831 (Ohio Ct. App. 2010).

Ohio does not recognize an implied warranty theory because to permit recovery under an implied warranty theory, without requiring proof of negligence, would make the builder-vendor an insurer. It also would disregard the harsh truth that unfortunate problems arise in real estate and in real structures that no prudence can avoid and that defy every reasonable skill. *Velotta*, 433 N.E.2d at 149–150; *Mitchem v. Johnson*, 218 N.E.2d 594, 598 (Ohio 1966). The law requires that the builder use ordinary care and skill. Performance in a workmanlike manner is determined by objective industry or trade standards. *Barton v. Ellis*, 518 N.E.2d 18 (Ohio Ct. App. 1986). The liability of the builder vendor for negligent construction is not limited to the original purchaser. *McMillan v. Brune-Harpenauu-Torbeck Builders, Inc.*, 455 N.E.2d 1276 (Ohio 1983).

Ohio courts recognize express warranties and determine their creation by examining the intent of the parties. *Bales v. Issac*, 2004 WL 1949419 (Ohio Ct. App. 2004) (unpublished opinion). Furthermore, an express warranty does not need to be in writing to be valid. *Id.* In *Bales*, the court noted that the builder "'guaranteed' his work and instructed the Bales to contact him if they 'ever' had 'any problems'" and such statements suggest there is a "triable issue regarding applicability of the discovery rule found in the Ohio Rev. Code § 1302.98(B)." *Id.* Furthermore, the court reasoned that the builder's oral warranty "explicitly extended to the future performance of the stucco, insofar as he assured the Bales that it applied to 'any problems' that 'ever' might arise." *Id.* As such, the court ruled that a cause of action for "the breach of warranty did not accrue until the breach was or should have been discovered." *Id.* (citing Ohio Rev. Code §1302.98(B) and finding plaintiffs' claim may not be time barred by § 1302.98(A)).

Oklahoma

The seller of a house that is sold during the construction phase impliedly warrants that the house will be completed in a workmanlike manner and be reasonably fit for occupancy except where the parties have an agreement to the contrary. *Jones v. Gatewood*, 381 P.2d 158 (Okla. 1963). Similarly, an implied warranty of habitability accompanies the sale of a new home by a builder-vendor. However, the builder-vendor is not required to construct a perfect home. In determining whether a home is defective, the test is reasonableness and not perfection. The duration of liability is likewise determined by the standard of reasonableness. *Jeanguneat v. Jackie Hames Constr. Co.*, 576 P.2d 761 (Okla. 1978); *Lucas v. Canadian Valley Vo-Tech School of Chickasha*, 824 P.2d 1140 (Okla. Ct. App. 1992).

The implied warranties of habitability and workmanlike construction apply to subsequent purchasers of the house. *Jaworsky v. Frolich*, 850 P.2d 1052 (Okla. 1992). In *Jaworsky*, the builder's potential liability in contract for breach of implied warranty ended on the fifth anniversary of the completion of the house. *Id.*; *Elden v. Simmons*, 631 P.2d 739 (Okla. 1981). A builder may disclaim the implied warranty by clear and unambiguous language in the contract. However, in the absence of an agreement to the contrary, the mere existence of an express warranty does not displace the obligations arising by operation of law under an implied warranty of habitability. *Bridges v. Ferrell*, 685 P.2d 409 (Okla. Ct. App. 1984).

Oregon

In the sale of a new house by a builder-vendor, an implied warranty assures that the house is constructed in a workmanlike manner and is fit for habitation. *Yepsen v. Burgess*, 525 P.2d 1019 (Or. 1974). *Yepsen* involved a defective septic tank and drain field system. In *Cabal v. Donnelly*, 727 P.2d 111 (Or. 1986), the plumbing and bathroom fixtures, equipment, and septic system were so defective that they rendered the house uninhabitable. In *Forbes v. Mercado*, 583 P.2d 552 (Or. 1978), the court found that the seller impliedly warranted the dwelling with a usable water system. However, when the builder agreed to build a specific house on the owner's lot for a price, implying a warranty for habitability was unnecessary, the trial court erred in submitting the implied warranty count to the jury. *Chandler v. Bunick*, 569 P.2d 1037 (Or. 1977). Importantly, the implied warranty covers defects that render a house uninhabitable, regardless of whether they could have been prevented by the exercise of reasonable care. *Forbes* at 553.

Pennsylvania

Pennsylvania expressly recognizes two warranties regarding builders-vendors of new residential construction: the warranty of habitability and the warranty of reasonable workmanship. *Elderkin v. Gaster*, 288 A.2d

771 (Pa. 1972). In *Elderkin,* the court held that the builder bears the risk that a home he built will be functional and habitable in accordance with contemporary and community standards. *See also Fetzer v. Vishneski,* 582 A.2d 23, 25 (Pa. Super. Ct. 1990). The warranty applies to a home built on the owner's lot. *Groff v. Pete Kingsley Building, Inc.,* 543 A.2d 128 (Pa. Super. Ct. 1988). In *Tyus v. Resta,* 476 A.2d 427 (Pa. Super. Ct. 1986), a case involving a leaky crawlspace, the court held that the warranties do not extend to defects of which the purchaser had actual knowledge, or which are or should be visible upon reasonable inspection. In *Quashnock v. Frost,* 445 A.2d 121 (Pa. Super. Ct. 1982), the court found that a crawl space beneath the house was not within reasonable inspection.

Pennsylvania extends warranties to subsequent purchasers. *Spivack v. Berks Ridge Corp. Inc.,* 586 A.2d 402 (Pa. Super. Ct. 1990). However, this is only in circumstances where the first purchaser never used or occupied the home. *Conway v. Cutler Group Inc.,* 99 A.3d 67 (Pa. 2014). Implied warranties may be waived by disclaimer language that is clear, prominent, and unambiguous. *Pontiere v. James Dinert, Inc.,* 627 A.2d 1204 (Pa. Super. Ct. 1993); *Ecksel v. Orleans Constr. Co.,* 519 A.2d 1021 (Pa. Super. Ct. 1987). Specifically, "habitability" and "reasonable workmanship" are needed to be specifically mentioned in any disclaimer. *Krishnan v. The Cutler Group,* 171 A.3d 856 (Pa. Super. Ct. 2017). In a case involving leaky skylights, the court ruled that a homeowner may recover as damages for breach of implied warranty of habitability, the cost of replacement for defective performance even if the cost is more than diminution in market value. *Fetzer,* 582 A.2d at 26–27 (Pa. Super. Ct. 1990).

Rhode Island

If a builder-vendor sells a house, either new or under construction, he or she implicitly warrants that the construction has been or will be done in a workmanlike manner and that the dwelling will be reasonably fit for human habitation. *Nichols v. R. R. Beaufort & Assocs., Inc.,* 727 A.2d 174, 177 (R.I. 1999) (quoting *Padula v. J. J. Deb-Cin Homes, Inc.,* 298 A.2d 529 (R.I. 1973)). *See also Sousa v. Albino,* 388 A.2d 804 (R.I. 1978). In *Nichols,* the Rhode Island Supreme Court discussed the public policy reason for applying implied warranties to home builders. "The applicability of the implied warranty is based upon the premise that, with respect to the sale of new homes, the purchaser has little choice but to rely upon the integrity and professional competence of the builder-vendor. The public interest dictates that if the construction of a new house is defective, its repair cost should be borne by the responsible builder-vendor who created the defect and is in a better economic position to bear the loss, rather than by the ordinary purchaser who justifiably relied upon the builder's skill." *Nichols*, 727 A.2d at 177.

An intervening tenancy may not preclude application of the implied warranties if it is not of such extended duration as to make an application of the warranties unreasonable. *Casavant v. Campopiano*, 327 A.2d 831 (R.I. 1974). Importantly, there is no privity requirement between contractors and subsequent homeowners. *Nichols*, 727 A.2d at 179. Although no rigid requirements for notification of defects exist, depending upon the circumstances, lack of notice may affect the credibility of a plaintiff's claim in greater or lesser degree. *Lacey v. Edgewood Home Builders, Inc.*, 446 A.2d 1017 (R.I. 1982). An action against a builder for breach of implied warranty is a contract action that can be brought more than 10 years after the home was completed. *Boghossian v. Ferland Corp.*, 600 A.2d 288 (R.I. 1991). The Rhode Island Supreme Court recently reaffirmed its earlier holding in finding 10 years was a reasonable period of time to discover a latent defect and that there is no distinction between original homeowners and subsequent homeowners with respect to how long a claim for breach of implied warranty of habitability remains actionable. *Mondoux v. Vanghel*, 243 A.3d 1039 (R.I. 2021).

Although a builder may exclude the implied warranties of workmanship and habitability in the purchase and sale agreement, the court will construe exclusionary provisions of doubtful meaning strictly against the builder. *Casavant*, 327 A.2d at 833.

South Carolina

South Carolina recognizes an implied warranty that a dwelling is fit for the purposes for which it is intended. *Rutledge v. Dodenhoff*, 175 S.E.2d 792 (S.C. 1970) (involving an improperly installed septic system). The protection of new home buyers is deep rooted and longstanding in South Carolina. *Damico v. Lennar Carolinas, LLC*, 437 S.C. 596 (2022).

In *Watson & Howell Builders v. Billingsley*, 425 S.E.2d 43 (S.C. Ct. App. 1992), the court observed that an obligation to perform in a workmanlike manner exists in every construction contract regardless of whether a house is built for speculation or is custom built. However, no warranty applies to a custom builder who is not also involved in the sale of the house. *Arvai v. Shaw*, 345 S.E.2d 715 (S.C. 1986). However, in *Kennedy v. Columbia Lumber & Mfg. Co., Inc.*, 384 S.E.2d 730 (S.C. 1989), the court recognized two distinct warranties: warranty of habitability and warranty of workmanlike service. That court also stated that a builder may not escape liability by refraining from selling the building.

Rather, a builder who contracts to construct a dwelling impliedly warrants that the work undertaken will be performed in a careful, diligent, workmanlike manner. *Kennedy*, 384 S.E.2d at 733. In *Lane v. Trenholm Building Co.*, 229 S.E.2d 728, 730 (S.C. 1976), the case involved breach of an implied warranty on a new home and the liability of the developer-seller who did not build the home.

The implied warranty for latent defects extends to subsequent purchasers for a reasonable period of time. *Terlinde v. Neely*, 271 S.E.2d 768 (S.C. 1980). If a party furnished plans and specifications for a contractor to follow in a construction job, he or she thereby impliedly warrants that the plans are sufficient for their intended purpose. *Tommy L. Griffin Plumbing & Heating Co. v. Jordan, Jones & Goulding, Inc.*, 463 S.E.2d 85, 89 (S.C. 1995).

A seller creates an express warranty when he or she makes an affirmation with respect to the product to be sold with the intention that the buyer shall rely on it in making the purchase. *Fields v. Melrose Ltd. P'ship*, 439 S.E.2d 283 (S.C. 1993).

A lender took ownership of an uncompleted house following financial difficulties of the original purchaser. The lender hired contractors and oversaw completion of the house, which was then sold. The purchaser sued the lender for construction defects claiming breach of the implied warranty of habitability. The lender argued that, as the lender, it was not subject to the implied warranty, and regardless of that fact, the sales contract included a disclaimer of the implied warranty of habitability.

The South Carolina Supreme Court ruled that under the doctrine of *caveat venditor*, which imposes on the vendor an implied warranty of a new house's habitability, the determining factor is not whether the defendant actually built the defective house, but whether he placed it, by initial sale, into the stream of commerce. A lender can be held liable to purchasers for a breach of the implied warranty of habitability if it is also a developer, and it becomes highly involved with construction in a manner that is not normal commercial practice for a lender. But, as a matter of first impression, the Court held that the principle of freedom of contract permits a party to effectively disclaim the implied warranty of habitability concerning a new house. *Kirkman v. Parex, Inc.*, 632 S.E.2d 854 (S.C. 2006).

In more closely examining the issue of disclaimers, the South Carolina Supreme Court found that certain disclaimers can be unconscionable. *Smith v. D.R. Horton, Inc.*, 790 S.E.2d 1 (S.C. 2016). A disclaimer of the implied warranty of habitability and a prohibition on the recovery of any monetary damages was found clearly one-sided and oppressive. *Id.* at 5.

South Dakota

In the sale of a new house, if the vendor is also the builder of the house for sale, the sale involves an implied warranty of reasonable workmanship and habitability that survives the delivery of the deed. The builder is not required to build a perfect house, and in determining whether a house is defective, the test is reasonableness and not perfection. The standard of reasonableness also determines the duration of the implied warranty. *Waggoner v. Midwestern Dev., Inc.*, 154 N.W.2d 803 (S.D. 1967). The presence of a Farmers Home Administration warranty did not preclude application of an implied warranty in *Sedlmajer v. Jones*, 275 N.W.2d 631 (S.D. 1979). The warranty extends only to a person who purchases a house from the builder-vendor of the house. However, a builder-vendor may be liable to a subsequent purchaser in an action based on negligence. *Brown v. Fowler*, 279 N.W.2d 907 (S.D. 1978).

In *Bunkers v. Jacobson*, 653 N.W.2d 732 (S.D. 2002), the South Dakota Supreme Court noted that, "a construction contractor who has followed plans or specifications furnished by the [customer], his architect, or engineer, and which have proved to be defective or insufficient, will not be responsible to the [customer] for loss or damage which results . . . solely from the defective or insufficient plans or specifications, in the absence of any negligence on the contractor's part, or any express warranty by him as to their being sufficient or free from defects." *Id.* at 741 (quoting *Reif v. Smith*, 319 N.W.2d 815, 818 (S.D. 1982)).

Tennessee

In Tennessee, a warranty is implied when the written contract is silent. The builder implies a warranty that the dwelling, together with all its fixtures, is sufficiently free from major structural defects and that it will meet the standard of workmanlike quality then prevailing at the time and place of construction. *Dixon v. Mountain City Constr. Co.*, 632 S.W.2d 538 (Tenn. 1982). The court in *Hays v. Gilliam*, 655 S.W.2d 158 (Tenn. Ct. App. 1983) declined to extend an implied warranty of habitability to a 20-year-old structure that had been reconstructed as an apartment building after being damaged in a fire. The builder-vendor and purchasers are free to contract in writing for a warranty with different terms and conditions, or expressly disclaim any warranty. In *Axline v. Kutner*, 863 S.W.2d 421 (Tenn. Ct. App. 1993), a provision in the sales contract stating, "one year builders warranty included," was not sufficient to avoid the implied warranty. Similarly, in *Dewberry v. Maddox*, 755 S.W.2d 50 (Tenn. Ct. App. 1988), the court held that a valid disclaimer must be in clear and unambiguous language and that the phrase "in good working order" was not sufficient to supplant the implied warranty. In *Bunch v. Cooper*, 1997 WL 600150 (Tenn. Ct. App. 1997) (unpublished opinion), the court recognized an express warranty of good workmanship and materials, with a clear disclaimer of any implied warranties. Importantly, the inclusion of a one-year builder's warranty is not sufficient to waive the warranties implied in law. *Campbell v. Teague*, 2010 W.L. 1240732 (Tenn. Ct. App. 2010).

The implied warranties in a contract of sale apply only to the initial purchaser. Dixon. 632 S.W.2d at 541–42; *Meyer v. Bryson*, 891 S.W.2d 223, 226 (Tenn. Ct. App. 1994), *but see Briggs v. Riversound Ltd. P'ship*, 942 S.W.2d 529 (Tenn. Ct. App. 1996). In that case, the court acknowledged that implied warranties are limited to the initial purchaser but held that a subsequent purchaser may maintain a negligence action against the builder. *Briggs*, 942 S.W.2d at 531.

Texas

The law is well established in Texas that the builder-vendor impliedly warrants that a building constructed for residential use is constructed in a good and workmanlike manner and is suitable for human habitation. *Humber v. Morton*, 426 S.W.2d 554 (Tex. 1968); *Wiggins v. Overstreet*, 962 S.W.2d 198 (Tex. Ct. App. 1998). The warranty of habitability is different from the warranty of good and workmanlike manner. The warranty of habitability requires that a house be safe, sanitary, and otherwise fit for humans to inhabit. *Centex Homes v. Buecher*, 95 S.W.3d 266 (Tex. 2003). Furthermore, it extends only to latent defects. *Id.* at 275; *Todd v. Perry Homes*, 156 S.W.3d 919, 921 (Tex. Ct. App. 2005).

The implied warranty of good and workmanlike manner has been defined as, "the manner in which an ordinarily prudent person engaged in similar work would have performed under similar circumstances." *Miller v. Spencer*, 732 S.W.2d 758 (Tex. Ct. App. 1987). *See Karmarath v. Bennett*, 568 S.W.2d 658 (Tex. 1978); *Evans v. J. Stiles, Inc.*, 689 S.W.2d 399 (Tex. 1985); *Melody Home Mfg. Co. v. Barnes*, 741 S.W.2d 349 (Tex. 1987); *Luker v. Arnold*, 843 S.W.2d 108, 115 (Tex. Ct. App. 1992). The implied warranty of good workmanship defines the level of performance expected when the parties fail to make express provisions in their contract and functions as a gap-filler whose purpose is to supply terms that are omitted from but necessary to the contract's performance; as a gap-filler, the parties' agreement may supersede the implied standard for workmanship, but the agreement cannot simply disclaim it. *Centex Homes*, 95 S.W. 3d at 274. Thus, Texas recognizes that implied warranties of good workmanship can be disclaimed by the contracting parties if the agreement provides for the manner, performance, or quality of desired construction. *Id.* at 274–75. However, the court held that the implied warranty of habitability could be waived only to the extent that defects are adequately disclosed. Thus, only in unique circumstances, such as when a purchaser buys a problem house with express and full knowledge of the defects that affect its habitability, should courts recognize a waiver of this warranty. *Id.* at 274. Therefore, an implied warranty of habitability could not be disclaimed generally. *Id.*

These implied warranties extend to subsequent purchasers. *Todd v. Perry Homes*, 156 S.W.3d 919 (Tex. Ct. App. 2005). In order for a plaintiff to prove a claim for breach of implied warranty of habitability, the plaintiff must show the property at issue is unsuitable for its intended use as a home and unfit for human habitation. *Id.* at 920 (citing *Centex Homes*, 95 S.W.2d at 273).

A developer owes an implied warranty to develop in a good and work-manlike manner. *Luker v. Arnold*, 843 S.W.2d at 116; *see also Parkway Co. v. Woodruff*, 857 S.W.2d 903 (Tex. Ct. App. 1993), modified and aff'd as reformed, 901 S.W.2d 434 (Tex. 1995). In the latter case, the court held that by marketing a subdivision as "master planned," the developer gave an implied warranty against the flooding of the purchaser's property that occurred when the developer diverted surface water across the property.

In 2003, the Texas Legislature enacted the Texas Residential Construction Commission Act, which created a Commission tasked with, among other responsibilities, adopting limited warranties and building performance standards. However, in 2009 the Commission was under sunset review and no legislation was passed to renew its existence. The Commission officially closed in 2010.

Express warranties are imposed by the agreements of parties to the contract. *Luker v. Arnold*, 843 S.W.2d 108 (Tex. Ct. App. 1992).

Utah

Until 2009, the state of the implied warranty law in Utah was unclear. Utah did not recognize implied warranties of habitability relating to construction of residential property and instead adhered to the traditional rule of *caveat emptor. Snow Flower Homeowners Ass'n v. Snow Flower, Ltd.*, 31 P.3d 576 (Utah Ct. App. 2001) (citing *American Towers Owners Ass'n, Inc. v. CCI Mechanical, Inc.*, 930 P.2d 1182, 1193–94 (Utah 1996)).

However, the case of *Davencourt at Pilgrims Landing Ass'n. v. Davencourt at Pilgrims Landing LC* changed everything. 221 P.3d 234

(Utah 2009). The court recognized Utah was in a minority of one when it came to excluding recovery under any implied warranty. As such, the court acknowledged that Utah recognizes a cause of action for breach of implied warranty of workmanlike manner and habitability. Like other states Utah explained that this does not require a contractor to deliver a perfect house. *Id.* at 253.

According to an earlier Utah Supreme Court decision, the common law doctrine of *caveat emptor* applied to the sale of real property, but under *Davencourt* the doctrine has been dismissed in the sale of new residential housing. However, it still prevails in the sale of used property whether they are residential or commercial in nature. *Utah State Medical Ass'n v. Utah State Employees Credit Union*, 655 P.2d 643 (Utah 1982). *See generally Beckstead v. Deseret Roofing Co., Inc.*, 831 P.2d 130 (Utah Ct. App. 1992) (involving a breach of express warranty to maintain roof in watertight condition for two years).

However, the Utah Supreme Court ruled that a developer owed no duty to a remote purchaser as a matter of law when the developer sold the land to a builder, and the property owner then sued the developer after the soil compacted. *Smith v. Frandsen*, 94 P.3d 919, 925–26 (Utah 2004). In reaching this decision, the court distinguished other state courts that did find developers liable to remote purchasers because in those cases, the facts established that "the developer was also the builder-contractor or otherwise included in the chain of title with no intermediate sophisticated purchaser." *Id.* at 926. The court recognized that its decision in *Frandsen* "requires contractors to be accountable, either directly or through explicit warranties from their predecessors in title, for the suitability of the land upon which they build." *Id.*

The court in *Frandsen* recognized the public policy reasons for creating exceptions to the doctrine of *caveat emptor* (let the buyer beware) that allowed expansion of builder contractor liability to encompass even remote purchasers. *Id.* As with initial residential construction consumers, subsequent homeowners typically possess no greater sophistication that would enable them to discover latent defects in the property. *Id.* at 926–27. However, in the case of subsequent purchasers possessing some unique insight or information regarding the property, courts will not extend liability to cover those subsequent purchasers. *Id.* at 927.

In 2005, the Utah Court of Appeals ruled that a developer had a duty to home purchasers to disclose an engineering report that revealed that the subsurface soil was extremely collapsible if the developer knew of the report prior to concluding the sale of the home. *Yazd v. Woodside Homes Corp.*, 109 P.3d 393, 396 (Utah Ct. App. 2005) (citing *Frandsen*, 94 P.3d at 926 (noting developer has a duty "to protect unsophisticated purchasers")). The issue of whether a duty exists is a question of law for the court to determine. *Yazd*, 109 P.3d at 396.

Vermont

Vermont law recognizes that the builder-vendor implicitly warrants to the buyer that the house is built in a good and workmanlike manner and is suitable for habitation. *Rothberg v. Olenik*, 262 A.2d 461 (Vt. 1970). The warranties apply to structural defects. *Id.* at 467. The implied warranty arises from the business of selling, rather than the business of manufacture. It applies where the seller builds a house expressly for resale and as part of a development plan. *Bolkum v. Staab*, 346 A.2d 210 (Vt. 1975). Privity is required for an implied warranty claim to be raised. *Long Trail House Condo. Ass'n. v. Engelberth Const., Inc.*, 59 A.3d 752, 761 (Vt. 2012).

The implied warranties apply only with respect to defects that were latent at the time of purchase. *Meadowbrook Condo. Ass'n v. South Burlington Realty Corp.*, 565 A.2d 238 (Vt. 1989) (finding that *Rothberg* requires neither perfection nor buyer satisfaction).

In *Heath v. Palmer*, 915 A.2d 1290 (Vt. 2006), homeowners sued the builder for latent construction defects on the grounds of a breach of the implied warranties of habitability and good workmanship. The builder contended that the claims fell outside of the one-year warranty provision of the express warranty policy provided to the owners and should be excluded. The Vermont Supreme Court ruled that exclusions or modifications of implied warranties must be conspicuous and unambiguous, and despite the contention of the builder, the duration limitation in the express warranty policy contained no reference to implied warranties, and therefore the implied warranties remained in effect. As to the duration of the implied warranties of habitability and good workmanship, the court ruled that duration is determined by a standard of reasonableness. *Id.* at 1293. In determining what is a reasonable duration, it stated that courts should look to such factors as the age of the home and its maintenance history, the nature of the defect and the extent to which it is discoverable through reasonable inspection, and the parties' expectations as to the reasonable durability of the defective structure. *Heath*, 915 A.2d at 1294.

Virginia

Pursuant to Virginia statutory law, the builder-vendor warrants to the purchaser that, at the time of transfer, recording the title, or the purchaser's taking possession, whichever occurs first, the dwelling together with all its fixtures is (a) sufficiently free from structural defects, so as to pass without objection in the trade; (b) constructed in a workman-like manner, so as to pass without objection in the trade; and (c) fit for habitation. *See* Va. Code Ann. § 55.1-357(C). The warranty extends for a period of one year, except that the warranty for the foundation of new dwellings extends for a period of five years. Va. Code Ann. § 55.1-357(F). Section 55.1-357 does not require homeowners to give a builder notice of an alleged defect in construction within the one-year warranty period. *Vaughn, Inc. v. Beck*, 554 S.E.2d 88 (Va. 2001). In *Beck*, the court considered whether the statute imposes any requirement on a homeowner that the homeowner give notice of a defect, within the statutory warranty period, before filing suit. *Id.* at 89. In reaching its decision, the court noted that § 55.1-357 changed the common law by creating certain statutory warranties. *Id.* at 90. As a result, the statute limits the warranties given to the provisions expressly stated or "necessarily implied" by the statute's language. *Id.* Therefore, the warranty extended for a one-year period, and, per the terms of the statute, a claimant must bring any action for breach within two years after the breach occurs. *Id.* at 91.

"A contract for sale may waive, modify, or exclude any or all express and implied warranties and sell a new home 'as is' only if the words used to waive, modify, or exclude such warranties are conspicuous, as defined by [Va. Code Ann. § 8.1A-201(b)(10)], set forth on the face of the contract[.]" Va. Code Ann. § 55.1-357(D). Specifically, the disclaimer language must be in capital letters and at least two points larger than the other text in the contract "that the dwelling is being sold 'as is.'" *Speier v. Renaissance Housing Corporation*, 58 Va. Cir. 90 (2001). In the case of new dwellings that have fire-retardant treated plywood sheathing, or other roof sheathing materials in lieu of fire-retardant treated plywood, the builder-vendor shall be deemed to have assigned the manufacturer's warranty to the purchaser at settlement. In so doing, the builder-vendor gives the purchaser a direct cause of action against the manufacturer of such roof sheathing. Va. Code Ann. § 55.1-357(G). A warranty to construct a townhouse in a good and workmanlike manner is collateral to the sale of the property. Such a warranty does not merge with the deed at closing and is enforceable. *Davis v. Tazewell Place Assocs.*, 492 S.E.2d 162 (Va. 1997).

Washington

Beyond the terms expressed in the contract of sale, the only recognized duty owing from a builder-vendor of a newly completed residence to its first purchaser is that embodied in the implied warranty of habitability, which arises from the sale transaction. *Berschauer/Phillips Constr.*

Co. v. Seattle Sch. Dist. No. 1, 881 P.2d 986 (Wash. 1994). Two prerequisites must exist for the implied warranty to arise from the sale of a new residential dwelling. First, the builder-vendor of the dwelling must be a commercial builder. Second, the unit must be built for sale rather than personal occupancy. *Atherton Condo. Apt. Owners Ass'n Bd. v. Blume Dev. Co.*, 799 P.2d 250 (Wash. 1990). *See also, Montgomery v. Engelhard*, 352 P.3d 218 (Wash. Ct. App. 2015). When a builder-vendor sells a new house to its first intended occupant, he or she impliedly warrants that the foundations supporting it are firm and secure and that the house is structurally safe for the buyer's intended purpose of living in it. *House v. Thornton*, 457 P.2d 199 (Wash. 1969). The warranty only extends to the first homeowners and not subsequent purchasers. *Carlile v. Harbour Homes, Inc.*, 194 P.3d 280 (Wash. Ct. App. 2008).

The courts have not precisely defined the entire realm of defects that are within the purview of this implied warranty. The implied warranty of habitability does not extend to mere defects in workmanship or impose upon a builder-vendor an obligation to construct a perfect house. However, claims are within the scope of the implied warranty of habitability if they arise from the builder-vendor's failure to comply with the applicable building code on fire resistance standards when constructing condominium units. *Atherton Condo.*, 799 P.2d at 259. The implied warranty of habitability does not provide recovery for defects in exterior, nonstructural elements near the home. These are things such as decks and walkways. *Stuart v. Coldwell Banker Commercial Group, Inc.*, 745 P.2d 1284 (Wash. 1987).

In *Burbo v. Harley C. Douglass, Inc.*, 106 P.3d 258, 263–64 (Wash. Ct. App. 2005), the court recognized that "an implied warranty requires (1) a plaintiff who is a first purchaser of (2) a new home from (3) a defendant whose business is building homes, and (4) defects that render the home unfit for its intended purpose." In this case, the builder asserted that the purchaser disclaimed and waived the implied warranty of habitability. *Id.* at 263. Washington courts do not favor warranty disclaimers. Thus, to disclaim an implied warranty, the disclaimer must be (a) conspicuous, (b) known to the buyer, and (c) specifically bargained for. *Id.; see also Griffith v. Centex Real Estate Corp.*, 969 P.2d 486 (Wash. Ct. App. 1998) (finding warranty limitation and disclaimer valid and enforceable) (citing *Southcenter View Condo. Owners' Ass'n v. Condo. Builders, Inc.*, 736 P.2d 1075 (Wash. Ct. App. 1986)).

Recently, in the Washington Court of Appeals, a split has occurred between divisions. Two cases, both involving the same facts, locations, injuries, and parties, were resolved using two fundamentally different standards for the statute of repose. *See Welsh v. Brand Insulations, Inc.*, 531 P.3d 265 (Wash. Ct. App. 2023); *Maxwell v. Atlantic Richfield Co.*,

476 P.3d 645 (Wash. Ct. App. 2020). Curiously, both courts thought they were applying the standard laid out in *Condit v. Lewis Refrigeration Co.*, 676 P.2d 466 (1984). That standard describes an "improvement upon real property" to be the construction of structural aspects of a building or integral systems that are a normal part of the kind of improvement required for the structure to function as intended. An "improvement upon real property" is a required prerequisite for the statute of repose to apply.

In 2020, the *Maxwell* court broadly interpreted and restated the rule from *Condit* as requiring a construction company to be "involved" in the construction of structural improvements or integral system(s). By contrast, in 2023, the *Welch* court adopted a much narrower interpretation, reasoning that for the construction statute of repose to apply, a contractor must show *all* their work relating to the building contributed to the construction of either a structural improvement or integral system, which is a much higher standard.

Until this conflict between divisions is settled, it is important for builders and contractors to understand how their work might be classified for purposes of the statute of repose. If they want to play it safe, they should look at their work through the lens of *Welsh* where all their work must relate to a structural improvement or integral system.

West Virginia

The concept of an implied warranty of habitability and fitness for a new home was initially adopted by the West Virginia Supreme Court in the case of *Gamble v. Main*, 300 S.E.2d 110 (W. Va. 1983). In West Virginia, the purchaser of a new home is entitled to an implied warranty of habitability or fitness requiring that the builder construct the dwelling in a workmanlike manner and that the property be reasonably fit for its intended use for human habitation. A home builder's implied warranty of habitability or fitness does not extend to adverse soil conditions that the builder is unaware of or could not have discovered by the exercise of reasonable care. *Gamble*, 300 S.E.2d at 115. Importantly, an overactive homeowner who becomes too involved in the construction process can render the implied warranties void. *See Sneberger v. Morrison*, 776 S.E.2d 156 (W. Va. 2015) (finding homeowner comparatively negligent for changes and modifications made to the home during construction).

The implied warranty of habitability and fitness for use as a family home may be extended to second and subsequent purchasers for a reasonable length of time after construction, but such warranties are limited to latent defects that are not discoverable by subsequent purchasers through reasonable inspection and that show up only after the purchase. *Sewell v.*

Gregory, 371 S.E.2d 82 (W. Va. 1988). Plaintiffs cannot bring a suit, in either contract or tort, against builders more than 10 years after construction. W. Va. Code Ann. § 55-2-6a.

Wisconsin

For many years, Wisconsin has followed the rule of *caveat emptor* with regard to new home purchases. *See, e.g., Dittman v. Nagel*, 168 N.W.2d 190 (Wis. 1969) (holding there are no implied warranties of quality in the sale of real estate). In fact, neither the Wisconsin Supreme Court nor the state legislature has recognized an implied warranty in a home purchased from a builder-vendor. Court opinions—both published and unpublished—have repeatedly said there are no implied warranties in new homes. For example, one unpublished Court of Appeals decision dismissed an action against a builder because the court determined that it lacked authority to create such a warranty. *Maltbey v. Nu Way Builders, Inc.*, 368 N.W.2d 847 (Wis. Ct. App. 1985) (unpublished opinion). Nevertheless, more than 10 years later, in another opinion, the Court of Appeals held that an implied warranty of fitness for the intended use exists in the contract for the sale of a home or condominium from a builder-vendor to a purchaser. *Shisler v. Crag Frank d/b/a CF Builders*, 582 N.W.2d 504, *6 (Wis. Ct. App. 1998) (unpublished opinion).

In 2002, a federal district court in Wisconsin noted that modern courts reject the rule of *caveat emptor. Riverfront Lofts Condo. Owners Ass'n v. Milwaukee/Riverfront Properties Ltd. P'ship*, 236 F. Supp. 2d 918, 927 (E.D. Wis. 2002). In *Riverfront Lofts*, the court ruled that implied in a developer's conveyance of condominium units are covenants of workmanlike performance and reasonable adequacy and that a developer cannot disclaim those covenants. In reaching this decision, the federal district court looked to both the Wisconsin statutes and case law outside the state for guidance. *Riverfront Lofts*, 236 F. Supp. 2d at 926 (noting at the date of the opinion 42 states have implied warranties of workmanlike performance and/or fitness for purpose in new home sales); *see also* Wis. Stat. Ann. § 706.10(7).

The court in *Riverfront* found that in Wisconsin statute § 706.10(7), a covenant is "implied when there is: (1) a conveyance from the grantor to the grantee, (2) 'evidencing a transaction under which the grantor undertakes to improve the premises' or 'to procure such improvement under grantor's direction,' (3) for the grantee's 'specified use and occupancy.'" *Riverfront*, 236 F. Supp. 2d at 928 (citing Wis. Stat. Ann. § 706.10(7)). The court concluded that the "purpose of the improvements in this case was to permit the building to be used for residences. Such anticipated use is sufficiently specified to trigger the implied covenant." *Id.* at 929. Furthermore, the court found its conclusion "buttressed by Wisconsin cases allowing purchasers of property intended to be used as a residence to recover from builder-vendors for negligent construction." *Id.* (citing *Oremus v. Wynhoff*, 123 N.W.2d 441 (Wis. 1963); *Fisher v. Simon*, 112 N.W.2d 705 (Wis. 1961)).

Wyoming

The rule of *caveat emptor* no longer protects the builder-vendor. Instead, if a vendor builds new houses for the purpose of sale, the sale carries with it an implied warranty that the house is constructed in a reasonably workmanlike manner and is fit for habitation. *Tavares v. Horstman*, 542 P.2d 1275 (Wyo. 1975). The state supreme court held that "consumer protection demands that those who buy homes are entitled to rely on the skill of the builder and that the house is constructed so as to be reasonably fit for its intended use." *Moxley v. Laramie Builders, Inc.*, 600 P.2d 733, 735 (Wyo. 1979); *Schepps v. Howe*, 665 P.2d 504, 510 (Wyo. 1983). The implied warranty extends to subsequent purchasers. *Moxley*, 600 P.2d 733; *see also Ortega v. Flaim*, 902 P.2d 199 (Wyo. 1995). Additionally, a builder-vendor may be liable for soil conditions under the theory of an implied warranty of fitness and/or habitability. *Farmer v. Rickard*, 150 P.3d 1185 (2007).

A builder-vendor breaches an implied warranty of habitability and fitness if the homeowner proves the existence of a minor construction defect and a resulting temporary injury to the property. The measure of damages is the cost of repair, but it also may include the diminished value of the property. *Deisch v. Jay*, 790 P.2d 1273 (Wyo. 1990). In *Deisch*, the court found the builder liable for breach of warranty because the owners experienced excessive humidity and dampness in their basements, which resulted in the development of mold and mildew and an offensive odor.

Wyoming allows waivers of implied warranties, including an implied warranty of habitability. For example, in *Greeves v. Rosenbaum*, 965 P.2d 669, 673 (Wyo. 1998), the Wyoming Supreme Court held that an "as is" clause in the homebuyer's contract was an effective waiver of any implied warranty, including habitability. *See also* Wyo. Stat. § 34.1-2-316 ("all implied warranties are excluded by expressions like 'as is,' 'with all faults' or other language which in common understanding calls the buyer's attention to the exclusion of warranties and makes plain that there is no implied warranty. . . ."). The court in *Greeves*, noted that provisions in the contract clearly notified the purchasers that they had the right to inspect, but the sale of the premises was "as is" and no implied warranties would be given. *Id.* at 673. Furthermore, the court said, "protection afforded to purchasers of a new home, however, does not go so far as to allow the purchasers to ignore *their* negotiated responsibilities." *Id.* (emphasis in original).

GLOSSARY

accrual. The point at which a claim comes into existence.

as is. In an existing condition, without modification.

best practices. Methods that are judged to be more effective or efficient than other methods and deemed superior.

boilerplate. An industry term for standard language that is not original to that particular contract.

builder-vendor. A contractor or developer who both constructs (or arranges the construction of) and sells a new residential dwelling.

caveat emptor. Let the buyer beware. A doctrine holding that purchasers buy at their own risk.

civil fraud. A knowing misrepresentation of the truth or concealment of a material fact to induce another to act to his or her detriment that can result in a monetary, noncriminal penalty.

closing. Final transaction between buyer and seller in which the conveyancing documents are concluded and the money and property transferred.

consequential damages. Losses that do not flow directly and immediately from an injurious act but that result indirectly from the act.

disclaimer. A statement that one is not responsible for or involved with something.

discovery rule. The point at which a claimant discovers a latent problem or defect or reasonably should have discovered it.

express warranty. A warranty deliberately created by the express words or actions of the maker.

implied warranty of fitness for a particular purpose. A warranty that is implied by law if a seller has reason to know of a buyer's particular purpose for the property, and the property is fit for such a purpose.

implied warranty of habitability. Premises carry an implied warranty that they are fit for human habitation and that they meet certain minimum standards for safe and sanitary housing.

implied warranty of merchantability. A warranty that is implied when the property is fit for the ordinary purpose for which property of that type is used.

implied warranty of workmanlike construction. A warranty implied by law that the work is performed in accordance with the accepted standards of construction for the time and place of performance.

latent defects. Defects that are hidden or not readily apparent from a reasonable inspection.

liability. The quality or state of being legally obligated or accountable; legal responsibility to another or to society, enforceable by civil remedy or criminal punishment.

limited warranty. A warranty that does not fully cover labor and materials for repairs.

liquidated damages. An amount contractually stipulated as a reasonable estimation of actual damages to be recovered by one party if the other party breaches the contract.

material breach. Such a breach of contract occurs when an action/activity is of significance or importance to the work or contract.

negligence. An illegal or wrongful act done either negligently or willfully, in which the actor owed the injured party some type of duty as imposed by law. A tort does not involve a breach of contract claim.

nonwarrantable conditions. Elements or events that a warranty does not cover.

notice and opportunity to repair (nor) statutes. Statutes that require a homeowner claiming a defect in construction to notify the builder of the problem and provide the builder an opportunity to repair the defect before filing suit.

privity. A relationship between parties based upon a contract.

public policy. Principles and standards regarded by the legislature or by the courts as being of fundamental concern to the state and the whole of society.

statute of limitation. Law that establishes a time for suing in court, based on when the claim accrued or when the injury occurred or was discovered.

statute of repose. The period after which a claimant can no longer bring an action in court. The period begins when a specific event occurs, regardless of whether an injury has occurred or whether a cause of action has accrued.

statutory. An obligation imposed legislatively.

subsequent purchaser. Purchaser of property who acquired the property after the initial sale; for example, the second or third purchaser of a home.

substantial completion. The point at which a building or remodeling project is ready for occupancy and can be used for its intended purpose, notwithstanding minor items to be completed or corrected; also referred to as substantial performance.

vendee. A purchaser or buyer.

vendor. A seller.

warranty coverage. The risks within the scope of the warranty.

warranty duration. Extent of time during which the warranty is valid.

INDEX

Note: Figures and tables are indicated by an *italicized* page reference.

G

general liability insurance, 43
Georgia
    cases and statutes, 101–102
    mandatory notice provisions, *47*
    warranty statutes, 63

H

habitability, 11, 13, 17, 18. *See also*
    implied warranty of habitability
    common-law warranty of, 97
    disclaimer of implied warranty of, 13,
      17, 18
Hawaii
    cases and statutes, 102–103
    mandatory notice provisions, *47*
    warranty statutes, 63
HUD. *See* Department of Housing and
    Urban Development

I

Idaho, cases and statutes, 103–104
Illinois
    case law, 7, 15, 17
    cases and statutes, 104–107
implied warranty, x, 5, 68
    disclaimers of, 11–16
    duration of, 13, *23, 25, 31*
    types of, 6
implied warranty of fitness for a
    particular purpose, 151
implied warranty of habitability, 6–9, 15,
    152
    disclaimer of, 13, 17, 18
    state cases and statutes and, 87–92,
      94–96, 98, 100–110, 112,
      116–121, 123–131, 135, 137–150
implied warranty of merchantability, 152
implied warranty of workmanlike
    construction, 6, 152
Indiana
    cases and statutes, 107–109
    implied warranty and, 6
    mandatory notice provisions, *48*
    statutory law, 13, *14*
    warranty statutes, 63–64

indirect damage claims, 3
informal dispute settlement mechanisms,
    77
inspections
    implied warranties and, 90–92, 97
    NOR statutes and, 43–44, 53
    spaces not within reasonable, 138
    structural defects and, 118
    subsequent purchasers and, 91,
      108–109, 148
    of work, 40
insurance, general liability, 43
International Residential Code, 41–42
Iowa
    case law, 8
    cases and statutes, 109–110

K

Kansas
    cases and statutes, 111–112
    mandatory notice provisions, *48*
Kentucky
    cases and statutes, 112–113
    mandatory notice provisions, *48*

L

latent defects, 8, 9, 12, 152
    significance of, 6
legislation
    Alternative Dispute Resolution Act, 57
    Federal Arbitration Act, 56
    Magnusson-Moss Warranty Act, *23–33*
    Notice and Opportunity to Repair, 43–52
Levittown, Pennsylvania, ix
liability, 152
    duration of, 11–12
    implied warranty, 5
liability insurance, 43
limited liability, duration of, 11–12
limited warranty, 2–3, 13, 152
    sample, *23–33*
liquidated damages, 152
litigation
    ADR as alternative to, 55
    construction-defect, 43
    prelitigation dispute resolution, 93